Please check out
this book by writing
your name in the
blue CIGE binder.
Thank you!

D0807416

THE FIRST TIME EFFECT

THE FIRST TIME EFFECT

The Impact of Study Abroad on
College Student Intellectual Development

Joshua S. McKeown

Published by
State University of New York Press, Albany

For information, contact State University of New York Press, Albany, NY
www.sunypress.edu

Production by Diane Ganeles
Marketing by Anne M. Valentine

Library of Congress Cataloging-in-Publication Data

McKeown, Joshua S., 1970–
    The first time effect : the impact of study abroad on college student
intellectual development / Joshua S. McKeown.
      p. cm.
    Includes bibliographical references and index.
    ISBN 978-0-7914-9359-5 (hardcover : alk. paper)
    ISBN 978-0-7914-9360-1 (softcover : alk. paper)
1. Foreign study. 2. College students—Intellectual life. 3. Intellect. I. Title.
    LB2375.M38 2009
    370.116—dc22
                                                                    2008014210

10   9   8   7   6   5   4   3   2   1

To International Educators Everywhere

Contents

Tables

Introduction

What are the benefits of studying abroad? Answers to this question have been limited and often unsatisfying, despite the long history of studying abroad in American higher education and remarkable increases in student participation in overseas academic programs. How *do we* know what, if any, positive outcomes are being achieved by the now over 200,000 students studying abroad each year? No president, provost, dean, or study abroad director would discourage the expansion of studying abroad on her or his campus, with most actively encouraging it, yet the kinds of inquiry and assessment that typically accompany first-year programs, academic curricula, living-learning communities, and other campus programs have largely been absent from study abroad.

One reason for the insufficiency of study abroad assessment efforts is the lack of consensus about what constitutes a quality study abroad program and what its educational objectives should be. We often disagree about whether studying abroad should be focused on language learning, cultural understanding, making the world a better place, career-relevant skills, country-specific knowledge, all of the above, or possibly something else. This disagreement makes assessment difficult, if not impossible. How can we assess if we are not sure what we are looking for?

We must add to this the considerable disagreement over whether short-term study abroad programs are "as good" as longer programs, and if not, why not? Students often find that they can better fit these shorter programs into their college careers, yet many campus leaders and study abroad professionals wonder aloud if students are gaining what they should from such programs, despite their popularity. Short-term programs often are faculty led, pulling the locus of control away from the study abroad office toward academic departments, which can complicate and confuse program

1

administration, not to mention any outcome assessment that the campus might wish to perform.

Studying abroad, despite its complexity, is generally viewed as a good thing for students to do and for campuses to invest in. Owing to its richness, and probably because it is such a multifaceted and challenging experience, campus leaders and professionals support it but do not always encourage closer scrutiny. It is a natural to support and expand as campuses push their students and faculty to a greater understanding of globalization and world awareness, and it is one of those rare academic programs for which there is often little or no organized opposition from boards, activists, or even disgruntled faculty members.

But this popular, almost untouchable, status has had, for some, an undesired effect. Studying abroad has high promotional value in admissions catalogues and Web sites; involvement in it, notably the international travel, can be a plum awarded to faculty members and other campus constituents, and it makes for great reading in alumni magazines. Interest in exotic and faraway places can make studying abroad irresistible to campus publicists, bringing with them the glare of the camera and the focus of the outside media. This "sex appeal" can, if not managed well, push studying abroad from being a serious academic endeavor occurring in another country dangerously close to being perceived of as little more than a fun, international adventure with little rigor sought or expected—in other words, "academic lite." This too can complicate assessment efforts, because the act of studying abroad can be seen by these outside eyes as a success unto itself, a kind of media darling that needs no further scrutiny, when in fact it is very much the kind of college program that should be reviewed for effectiveness and impact.

For students, studying abroad is almost always an eye-opening, once in a lifetime experience. Study abroad advisors and faculty members often love talking to returning students, seeing the changes in them and how much they have grown—observations that have been historically rooted and passed on in the study abroad field since its inception (Hoffa, 2007). Returning students can seem more sophisticated, more focused on what is important and less on the petty and the trivial. "She seems more mature," a faculty colleague will say. "They're a pleasure to have in class," will say another, "because they bring a perspective the others don't." "They see the big

picture." This unmeasured change that we detect can be both grati-
fying and maddening: *What* is this change, and *how* can we document it so our colleagues and constituencies can see it too?

Too often, dedicated and well-meaning international educators are left feeling overwhelmed, and perhaps a little hollow,
regarding the complexity of trying to understand and assess all that
is happening in their students' study abroad programs while continuing to run programs for the next group coming down the pike.
Financial pressures to expand enrollments, campus pressures to
diversify offerings, academic pressures to enrich the curriculum, and
mission-driven pressures to internationalize serve as a frenzied
backdrop, pushing us to do more abroad while often not identifying
how studying abroad specifically fits into the college's life and
specifically *what* students are gaining from the experience.

Pausing for a moment to consider the contrary perspective,
perhaps those questions are inappropriate. Perhaps it is unrealistic to
expect to capture the essence of studying abroad, and its incalcula-
ble benefits to students, with quality jargon and assessment metrics.
Perhaps we should leave studying abroad alone, in a space longed for
by purists and resented by dissatisfied consumers, as an untouchable,
well-liked college program, immune from scrutiny and cherished by
all. If this were possible, then our lives would be wonderful indeed.
But this is not the case.

Study abroad assessment efforts are growing but are still
largely a work in progress. This book is an attempt to contribute to
the vibrant and accelerating discussion about study abroad outcomes
assessment in American higher education. In particular, I introduce
and explain the results of a research project I conducted that sought
answers to some of these long-asked questions. Particularly I
explain, and possibly introduce, to the reader one outcome measure,
intellectual development, that previously has not been applied to
studying abroad in such a thorough manner. Intellectual development measures a student's ability to think in complex ways, to view
and interpret information in a diverse and pluralistic world, to
embrace multiple and relativistic viewpoints instead of rigid "black-
or-white" arguments, and ultimately to commit to beliefs and ways
of thinking that reflect both a more sophisticated intellect and a
more responsible worldview.

The chapters that follow provide the detail, support, and context for my findings that studying abroad, for some students, is associated with gains in intellectual development relative to their peers. These findings show that students for whom studying abroad was their *first meaningful international experience* made gains in their intellectual development not seen in their peers. Other variables of common interest to the study abroad field, such as the language of the study abroad country and the degree of cultural immersion, did not have such an impact. Only the degree to which the study abroad experience was the first serious international encounter mattered.

I approach this book mainly as a higher education practitioner who is steadily passionate about studying abroad. This work is grounded in both theory and practice, reflecting my belief that without each, as the saying goes, we do our work blindly and without meaning. Theory helped me frame the research questions, ascertaining as sharply as possible what I was studying and why it was important to know. My practice as a higher education administrator helped shape the study itself, both in terms of methodology and style, allowing it to be completed properly within a reasonable period of time and, hopefully, presented in a manner that is useful and approachable.

In chapter 1 I introduce the current state of studying abroad and how the study presented in this book can contribute to what we know about the effect of studying abroad on today's college students. I provide data, trends, and some analysis on how studying abroad has evolved recently and why now is a vital time to study it further, regardless of campus culture or past experiences with international study. Chapter 1 also provides the reader with some background on college student development theory, intellectual development in particular, and how this theory is germane to studying abroad. Selected experiences from student participants and study abroad professionals bring to life some of this theory.

In chapter 2 I provide a thorough but not cumbersome review of literature related to the topics of study abroad research and student intellectual development, and I explain more fully why those two themes should be joined in the manner of this study. My intent is to weave the literature into the book's theme of intellectual development on studying abroad in a natural, seamless way. While some of the literature sources are well-known in higher education, and others are well known in the study abroad field, they previously have not been synthesized in this way.

The reason I have chosen this approach is that study abroad research has tended to reside outside of the higher education mainstream. Top higher education graduate programs often do not focus on topics in international education or studying abroad, just as campuses routinely tout studying abroad but rarely devote time and attention to assessing it in the same way they do general education requirements or first-year programs. Therefore, I seek to bridge these worlds. I also discuss in chapter 2 that study abroad research, to date, has important gaps, some of which I seek to fill with this work.

An overview of my research study methods and procedures is provided in chapter 3. In particular, some space is given to the survey instrument used in the study (the Measure of Intellectual Development, or MID), how I used it, and some specifics about the students participating in the study and the programs in which they took part. Without this information, it will not be possible for readers to see how the research and the findings apply to their situation. I am guided in my writing by how often, as higher education professionals, we are enticed to buy into simplistic "just add water" approaches that deny our own institution's unique character and traditions. My hope is that this research study and the accompanying results are viewed credibly and seriously, all the while fully grounded in the day-to-day realities of life on campus.

In chapter 4 I detail the results of the study. This is a crucial chapter that explains that not all students showed a statistically significant gain in intellectual development after one semester of studying abroad, and why that was likely the case. This overall finding should not surprise us, and should not, in my view, be seen negatively. In fact, many educators would likely be skeptical of any study showing dramatic, universally positive results after only one semester of anything. Education is a process, after all, and our students are at different stages of learning and development.

However, some students did show gains in intellectual development relative to their peers. These students were the ones who had not traveled abroad for any meaningful period of time prior to studying abroad. In other words, it was precisely those students who had lacked meaningful international exposure who seemed to benefit most from studying abroad.

This finding is simple and complicated at the same time. On the one hand, it is not surprising, since international travel involves unique challenges, stress, and joy, and therefore it changes students in ways that may affect their intellectual development. But, on the other hand, it is noteworthy that this reaction does not seem to have a cumulative effect. The impact on intellectual development was evident only in those students for whom studying abroad was their first trip abroad for a meaningful period of time. For this study I grouped students who had taken very short international trips, such as a day trip to Canada or spring break in Cancun, with those with no prior international travel. That grouping is especially important, since the time period of study was the semester study abroad program. The findings reveal that students who had been abroad for as little as 2 weeks showed patterns of intellectual development more similar to peers who had been abroad for months or years than to those who had not been abroad at all. This suggests to me that something profound happens during that first international encounter. With this book I hope to shed light on what that profound happening is, and how studying abroad, even for a short period of time, can contribute to it.

In chapter 5 I conclude and discuss my research in specific ways that advocate for studying abroad as an activity that can foster college student intellectual development. My argument is that since college students tend to cite desire for travel and adventure as a primary motivator for studying abroad, colleges and universities should deliberately harness their students' interest in travel by designing as many study abroad programs as possible, including short-term programs, in order to satisfy this student demand without worrying erroneously that these programs are of little academic value. We should rely on our proven ability to ensure academic rigor and integrity on study abroad programs while respecting our students' increasingly intrepid desire to travel and experience the other in many places, and for as much or as little time, the only limits being what our collective creativities and talents permit us.

While this study suggests that any travel abroad for a meaningful length of time could produce significant intellectual development for the first-time sojourner, I argue that the unique combination of academic structure and international experience makes a compelling case for studying abroad as a worthy activity not only for enhancing our students' cultural competency and international understanding but also for deliberately fostering intellectual development for those first-time sojourners. College and university leaders, as well as study abroad professionals, can use this information to present studying abroad not only as an opportunity to gain international knowledge and possibly language skills but also as a credit-bearing way to foster intellectual development that can carry over into our students' other courses and academic programs overall.

The findings presented in this book will be especially useful in encouraging short-term study abroad programs. Higher education for too long has agonized over whether or not short-term faculty-led programs, including internship and service programs, were academically sound. This bias toward traditional semester or year-long programs stems from the very well-meaning belief shared by most faculty members and study abroad professionals, myself included, that more is better when it comes to studying abroad. However, I will make the argument that studying abroad for a short time is better than no study at all. Students are choosing to study in short-term programs more often every year, thus those lasting less than one semester are now the majority of study abroad programs. Higher education and the study abroad profession must respect this trend. My research provides the study abroad profession and the larger higher education community with the encouragement that these short-term programs can have a positive impact on students, an endorsement recently shared by the National Survey of Student Engagement, or NSSE (NSSE, 2007).

It must be remembered that this research does not address the linguistic and cultural gains of studying abroad. My reasons for not focusing on these areas, as established in chapter 1, are, namely, that these approaches are already fairly well researched and, more importantly, they are less relevant to today's college experience. Regarding language learning abroad, it is less relevant to focus there, because English-language destinations are very popular. Roughly 25% of American study abroad students do so in the United Kingdom (UK) and Australia. Further, short-term programs are as brief as 1 week, providing little opportunity for demonstrable gains in language ability in non-English-speaking countries. Concerning cultural and country-specific knowledge, again, since short-term programs are now the majority of study abroad programs, it is not always possible or realistic for students to realize demonstrable gains in cultural ability or country-specific knowledge with such little exposure and involvement.

Indeed, the *first time effect* that I describe focuses on intellectual development in our students instead of traditional linguistic and cultural measures, because by focusing there we free ourselves to embrace nontraditional study abroad programs, short-term study abroad programs, and innovative topics and faculty-led approaches, such as a biology class to the Brazilian Amazon or a comparative education course in Benin and France (two courses incorporating short-term study abroad programs recently offered at my institution, the State University of New York at Oswego). These programs may or may not incorporate a deliberate component of language, cultural learning, or country-specific knowledge. For these reasons, exploring new ways of assessing study abroad programs, such as measuring intellectual development, is relevant.

Particularly relevant to the society and world that the next generations are inheriting is the likelihood of a culturally diverse encounter. Whether as immigrants or as travelers, or simply as neighbors in diverse communities, the possibility of enduring life without cultural complexity is remote. I discuss in chapter 5 the intellectual impact of such encounters, drawing from sources in psychology that describe why, and under what scenarios, intense cultural experiences can lead to cognitive change and growth. It is normal and human to attempt to resist these disruptive influences, especially in adulthood, but intense disruptions such as the shock of an international encounter are known to facilitate intellectual development if properly supported in the manner of a well-run study abroad program.

I further discuss and argue in chapter 5 ways to include deliberate reflective and experiential components into study abroad programs to strengthen our programs' capacity to provide meaningful experiences for participating students, whether studying abroad for 1 week or for 1 year. Seen this way, there is no bad study abroad program per se. There may be bad teaching or poor-quality delivery, but that is no different from higher education on campus.

I conclude that studying abroad is an activity that warrants full-throated encouragement for as many students as possible. It involves meaningful, credit-bearing experiences that allow students to gain from the subject matter and destination country, with the added benefit of producing demonstrable gains in intellectual development for first-time sojourners.

CHAPTER 1

A New Look at Study Abroad

(T)he personality does not just unfold automatically
according to a plan of nature. Whatever the stage of
readiness in the personality, further development will not
occur until stimuli arrive to upset the existing equilib-
rium and require fresh adaptation.
—Nevitt Sanford, "Where Colleges Fail"

One of the central tenets of college student development literature is
that students change during their college years (Baxter Magolda,
1992; Chickering, 1969; Kohlberg, 1971; Perry, 1968). While students are at different developmental levels and at different times
while in college, the challenge and support concept of college student
development put forth by Sanford (1962) applies throughout the college years. The "challenge and support" concept refers to the optimal
conditions under which college students grow and develop. The
appropriate amount of challenge can provide potentially growth-pro-
ducing conditions as the student encounters complexity, ambiguity,
diversity, and other stressful experiences that require new ways of
coping. Too little challenge may not provide conditions conducive to
growth and development. The appropriate amount of support can
provide a degree of familiarity for the student, as well as the attention, caring, and empathy necessary for tackling other challenges in
life. Too little support can produce unhealthy feelings of being overwhelmed, overstressed, and dissatisfied, and even illness and exit
from the environment (Huebner & Lawson, 1990; Tinto, 1993).

Studying abroad is an academic experience, whether short
term (as short as 1 week) or longer (up to a full academic year), during which students physically leave the United States to engage in
college study, cultural interaction, and more in the host country. It
may include foreign language study, residing with a foreign host

11

family, internships, and service. Studying abroad, and its impact on student development, is a subject with a worthwhile, but limited, body of research.

My study investigated the impact of studying abroad on one measure of college student development (intellectual development) on undergraduate students during one study abroad semester. This research aimed to measure college students' intellectual reasoning ability prior to and at the end of their study abroad semester using the MID (Moore, 1990), an existing instrument done in essay format. The information gathered from students taking this instrument was combined with demographic data, data defining the type of study abroad program experienced, and data provided by students describing their activities during their study abroad semesters.

Measuring the impact of studying abroad is difficult, because the experience itself is complicated, and many factors can shape a study abroad experience for the student involved. As one student participant in this study reported at the end of her semester in Ireland:

> This study abroad experience has taught me a great deal about myself as a learner and as a person. I have had the opportunity to work with other people from the United States but also with many other Europeans as well. I have learned a great deal about how the world views the United States, and the everyday decisions it makes as a world leader. I have been forced to become a more open and accepting individual (a characteristic I value greatly) and am pleased to say that I know more about the world, but also found out how little I did know before this experience.
>
> I worked in a group atmosphere with three Irish students, one Canadian student, and one Swedish student. We all had to overcome stereotypes about cultures to work together. I am pleased to say that I value the relationships I have made with students from other cultures and learned a great deal about everyday life and learning from these students.

This student describes her own growth and learning while abroad in a varied and rich way. It was part location, part cohort, part distance from home, part self-awareness, part cultural, part personal, and much more. Any one of these aspects of the study abroad experience would be complex to study, making the whole endeavor a tough nut to crack.

One reason for this complexity of analysis is the various program options available, reflecting the uniqueness and diversity of American colleges and universities themselves. Higher education researchers and leaders consistently cite the importance of undertaking initiatives within the cultural context of a particular campus as a key ingredient of its potential for success. Birnbaum (1988), for example, believed that approaches or policies fruitful for one institution may in fact be harmful for another; Shaw (1999) stated that frustration and failure can result if the values, vision, and people of the institution are ignored. What these observations share is the suggestion that any attempt at serious study abroad assessment, like the organization of study abroad programs themselves, must be grounded in campus culture without a one-size-fits-all approach (McKeown & Nekritz, 2006).

Students study abroad in study centers mostly with other U.S. college students, and they study directly in foreign university settings, as well as in programs that combine the two. Students live in culturally rich environments, such as host families and international living centers, and live with other U.S. students in program-arranged apartments or residence halls. They study and live abroad in foreign language countries as well as English language countries, and some seek out and take part in activities and experiences that immerse them into the local cultural milieu, while others spend most of their time socializing with U.S. friends, traveling, and taking part in touristic activities. These variables in the study abroad experience can make any outcome of studying abroad difficult to measure.

Similarly, intellectual development is a complicated process influenced by many factors. It is possible that something this complicated may not be possible to measure over one semester's duration, even if the activities and program experienced may have a direct or delayed impact. However, a well-run semester study abroad program has many intentionally designed components that provide a suitable venue in which to study intellectual development in college students.

My study was built upon previous ones that demonstrated that studying abroad can have some positive impact on college student learning and personal growth. In particular, the work of Carlson, Burn, Useem, and Yachimowicz (1990) and Citron (1996) will be discussed. These researchers found that study abroad students show an enhanced ability to understand complexity, one aspect of intellectual development, and that the differences in study abroad program structure and experience can impact the outcomes of study abroad for the students involved. Program structure and experience are dimensions explored in this research study. This study also is based on the premise that as study abroad participation rates and the diversity of program offerings are rising nationally (Institute of International Education, 2004), more research is needed on the impact of studying abroad on college students generally, and specifically research examining particular variables in program type important to studying abroad (Engle & Engle, 2003). The need for more analytical study abroad research, in particular research that is less anecdotal and descriptive, also has been cited (De Wit, 1997; Van Hoof & Verbeeten, 2005).

Problem

As colleges and universities seek to increase the number of students studying abroad and expand the number and type of study abroad programs offered, there should be a concurrent investigation into the effect that these programs are having on participating students. Institutions of higher education, among other objectives, seek to enhance students' global awareness and competence, an area where studying abroad has been shown to be effective (Douglas & Jones-Rikkers, 2001; Drews, Meyer, & Peregrine, 1996; Sharma & Mulka, 1993; Sutton & Rubin, 2004). But colleges and universities also have an interest in enhancing students' understanding of diversity, critical thinking ability, and ethical conduct. Enhancing a student's intellectual reasoning ability can contribute to these important competencies (Kohlberg, 1971; Mines, King, Hood, & Wood, 1990; Perry, 1968). Understanding how studying abroad impacts intellectual development can help colleges and universities justify the increased focus on studying abroad in new ways, as well as demonstrate the ways in which studying abroad contributes to student success.

Background

Students in the United States are studying abroad in increasing numbers. A record number of over 200,000 U.S. college students chose to study abroad in 2004–2005, a figure that has quadrupled over the past 20 years, according to the Institute of International Education, or IIE (IIE, 2006). Calls to increase study abroad participation and greater global competence come from many sources, both inside and outside the academy (Marcum, 2001; NAFSA, 2003; Syracuse University, 2001; U.S. Department of Education, 2000). Colleges recognize the responsibility of preparing students for the realities of the world, to learn about other peoples and cultures, and to do so in an appropriate, respectful manner. The student affairs profession also has been encouraged to globalize, both to prepare students for the complex, global economy and the society they are about to enter and to reinforce tolerance, respect for diversity, and understanding of complex global social, economic, political, and environmental challenges for the benefit of the rest of campus (Christie & Ragans, 1999). Studying abroad is positively associated with these desired outcomes.

Still, studying abroad is not for everyone. It is only one of many activities in which college students can participate, and it is sometimes difficult to include during a demanding, multifaceted undergraduate education. It can be expensive and frightening, and not every professional career can benefit directly from the language and cultural skills typically learned through studying abroad. There are at least two major reasons to study this type of student experience. The first has to do with the arrival of the so-called global village. As the late Clark Kerr, former president of the University of California system, stated:

> Since the late 1970s, the theme of a "global perspective" has emerged. . . . (T)he notion of a "global village" has replaced the older international dream of a "world order," and emphasizes the interdependence of all the peoples of the world. (1985, p. xiv)

The cultural and linguistic challenges of international business, the competitive pressures caused by globalization of the economy (Koveos & Tang, 2004), the ongoing impact of 9/11, and the role played by the United States in the larger world (Ferguson, 2001), the ecological impact of global warming and other international environmental challenges, and technologically facilitated Internet and telephonic communications are all evidence of global interdependence that today's U.S. college students cannot avoid.

Today we know that, at the beginning of the 21st century, activities and interactions that once were assumed to occur within the borders of one state are increasingly occurring across national boundaries. Employment, business relationships, professional associations, and social and family connections are some examples (Opello & Rosow, 2004). This ongoing process of globalization, which has been defined as "the complex of economic, technological, ecological, and cultural structures that are emerging on a global scale which ignore or deny the relevance of any state's territory" (Poggi, 1990, p. 117), has led to new challenges to the notion of a national identity and new pressures on the individual to engage competently in the free flow of ideas, commerce, and communications across national boundaries (Opello & Rosow, 2004). To the extent that studying abroad is viewed as a way to prepare U.S. students to engage in this more global society, it warrants further examination.

The second major reason to examine studying abroad, and the direction this book is taking, is its effect on college student development. As Sanford stated:

> . . . the personality does not just unfold automatically according to a plan of nature. Whatever the stage of readiness in the personality, further development will not occur until stimuli arrive to upset the existing equilibrium and require fresh adaptation. (1967, p. 54)

For the student engaged in a study abroad experience, almost everything is new and presents a challenging opportunity to learn. Regardless of the structure of the study abroad experience, its duration, or its quality, an American student placed in a foreign environment must navigate through new customs and practices to accomplish everyday tasks, both basic and complex. Ordering breakfast, catching the bus, paying for goods and services, and, of course, communicating with and understanding people all fall under the category "stimuli requiring fresh adaptation." As one student participant in this study stated about his semester in Madrid, Spain:

> From the moment that I arrived in Madrid for the orientation, I knew that this experience was going to change my views on the world. Even in a big city like Madrid it was evident that the country of Spain was extremely different than New York. This experience has helped me to realize what is inherently different is not always bad. . . . Additionally, I do think that most of my learning was done outside the classroom and was influenced by outside events. Although I took a class in Spanish language I feel as though most of my learning of the language was done by simply talking to native Spaniards.

This student, in retrospect, knew that some of his biggest learning opportunities occurred in the daily charms and challenges of life in Madrid, and from his actual conversations with the Spanish people. Writing shortly after his spring 2004 semester abroad, he specifically cited how experiencing the Madrid terrorist bombings in the Atocha train station on March 11, 2004, along with his fellow Madrileños, was important to him:

> My learning from these events was centered around the reaction to the attacks. During the day after the attacks the Spanish people took to the street to protest and express sympathy for those murdered. This did not happen in the United States after September 11. Neither did the new government react by taking away the civil liberties of the citizens. Furthermore, the Spaniards themselves did not seem to be living in fear of another attack; they simply went on with their lives, which did not happen here in America after September 11, and which is still not happening today.

While reacting to a terrorist attack is, thankfully, still not a common experience either in the United States or abroad, this student's experience exemplifies vividly how important those actual moments of cultural interaction are in providing a catalyst for learning and growth on the part of study abroad students.

As mentioned earlier, studying abroad is growing in popularity (IIE, 2005). While it has grown in enrollment numbers, it also has been changing, as can be seen in several recent findings. First, studying abroad has become increasingly appealing to students with different majors. For example, in 1986, social science, humanities, and foreign language majors accounted for 56% of study abroad participants. By 2002, those majors accounted for less than 45% of study abroad participants. During the same time, business, physical science, health science, math, engineering, and computer science majors increased from 19% of study abroad participants to 33% (IIE, 2003). Second, the destination of study abroad programs is becoming more diverse. In 1986, Europe accounted for nearly 80% of study abroad participation but in 2002, only 63%. Latin America, Asia, Oceania, and multiple destination study abroad programs increased from 14% to 33% of all study abroad participation during that same time (IIE, 2003). While we know something about what motivates students to study abroad, and what concerns they may have (Martin & Rohrlich, 1991; McKeown, 2003; Schroth & McCormack, 2000), a deeper understanding of the benefits to students studying abroad is needed.

These changes in participation patterns suggest that new methods of measuring what is happening to students who study abroad should be considered. Research on studying abroad as a vehicle to enhance language acquisition (Citron, 1995; Rivers, 1998; Thot, 1998) and international understanding (Douglas & Jones-Rikkers, 2001; Drews, Meyer, & Peregrine, 1996; Sharma & Mulka, 1993; Sutton & Rubin, 2004) is available. However, as study abroad programs attract a lower proportion of foreign language majors, measuring gains in language acquisition is becoming less applicable to study abroad students overall. Likewise, as short-term programs, sometimes as short as several weeks or less, now account for the majority share of study abroad participation (IIE, 2006), measuring demonstrable gains in country-specific knowledge, cultural understanding, and international awareness could be considered less relevant.

The need for additional research on the impact of studying abroad has been identified within the study abroad profession

(NAFSA, 2003; The Forum on Education Abroad, 2003) and by international education researchers (De Wit, 1997; Van Hoof & Verbeeten, 2005), and the benefits of studying abroad have been questioned from outside the study abroad profession (Feinberg, 2002; Roochnik, 2001). The common question in these calls for greater understanding about study abroad is: Are students benefiting from study abroad programs in ways that are measurable and useful? A broader understanding of what is happening to students developmentally while abroad will contribute both to study abroad practitioners and to the field of higher education research.

Student Development during Study Abroad

As both a researcher and a professional coordinating study abroad programs, I am concerned about the general topic of growth and development that occurs during the study abroad experience. Intellectual development is one facet of college student development; it is an evolving process and occurs in interaction with the environment (King, 1990). Intellectual development (or cognitive development) is typically defined as the process during which the individual actively attempts to make sense out of her or his experience. This attempt at making meaning out of experience often requires that the individual construct new ways of understanding life, an internal logic that allows her or him to interpret events in a manner that is explainable and understandable (King, 1978).

Intellectual development is one facet of college student development and is important to the field of higher education because studying changes in students' intellectual development allows educators to determine whether a college education, as well as its separate components and programs, is providing good opportunities for appropriate challenge and growth. Studying abroad involves international travel, cultural unfamiliarity, and often foreign languages; it is the type of experience that is challenging and sometimes uncomfortable, what Kim (1988) calls the "adversarial nature of the cross-cultural adaptation process" (p. 144). Consequently, studying abroad could provide a meaningful venue in which to examine the impact of these experiences on students' meaning-making structures. The challenges that are typically a part of studying abroad could provide stress, diversity, ambiguity, and unfamiliarity—what Huebner and Lawson (1990) refer to as the mismatch between the environment and the student's current coping skills that often facilitates intellectual developmental growth.

Optimal Conditions for Student Development to Occur

Baxter Magolda (1992) argued that intellectual development can be facilitated by well-structured, intentionally implemented academic and co-curricular activities. Broader student development research shows that experiences outside the classroom can be associated with student learning and personal development (Kuh, 1995); that moral development can be facilitated by deliberate activities such as the Defining Issues Test (Rest, 1980) and morally focused, teacher-led discussions (Kohlberg, 1980); that on-campus leadership education and involvement in leadership programs can facilitate in students an appreciation of desired attitudes, such as civic responsibility and multicultural awareness (Cress, Astin, Zimmerman-Oster, & Burkhardt, 2001); that psychosocial outcomes can be influenced by students' choices of activities and effort during college (Martin, 2000); and that factors such as exposure to cultural, religious, racial, and social diversity during college (Pascarella, Palmer, Moye, & Pierson, 2001) and the characteristics of the college attended (Flowers & Pascarella, 1999) can influence outcomes such as critical thinking.

In the field of study abroad research, Citron (1996) found that program structure, particularly the lack of a program director, organized orientation, and guided learning activities, negatively affected cultural integration in the host country. Rivers (1998) discovered that gains in foreign language ability do not always improve when a student participates in a family home stay when studying abroad. And Marion (1980) found that certain political attitudes in students can be influenced by the study abroad program country and program structure. These findings illustrate the complexity of studying abroad, that its outcomes go beyond language and culture skills, that we should be careful in making assumptions about its benefits, and that more than a cursory review of it as a subject matter is overdue.

The research cited earlier shows that certain types of experiences can have an impact on student development and other outcomes in on-campus settings. Further, it shows that deliberately organized and implemented experiences are preferable to more passive ones for fostering student development in on-campus settings and for program outcomes in studying abroad. Together this research suggests that study abroad programs would benefit from research designed to measure student developmental outcomes in similar ways.

Student development differs from maturation in that research on student maturation, such as Heath's model of maturing, holds that students will adapt to new circumstances and will over time become stable, autonomous beings able to resist bias and disruptive influences (Widick, Parker, & Knefelkamp, 1978). This philosophical approach suggests passivity: things simply happen, and students adjust to what is happening in order to survive. Similarly, research on international experiences often has focused on certain adjustment behaviors, such as skills acquisition and the adoption of social roles (Furnham & Bochner, 1986), and the largely uniform development of second culture coping skills (Adler, 1975) instead of intellectual development. A student who is developing intellectually is undergoing a process of upward developmental movement that allows for a greater capacity to understand and make meaning out of both the experience at hand and future ones. This process is not assured and occurs best when done actively in a supportive environment with appropriately challenging activities and programs (Knefelkamp, Widick, & Parker, 1978).

As stated previously, there is reason to believe that students develop during the college years, and that certain activities facilitate this development. This study seeks to understand whether studying abroad is one of the types of experiences that facilitate student intellectual development. The impact of studying abroad on student development is an area where some interesting, but limited, literature exists (Kauffmann & Kuh, 1984; Kauffmann, Martin, Weaver, & Weaver, 1992). Using Perry's (1968) scheme for describing intellectual development during college, a scheme that has not been applied to study abroad students in this way, I set out to learn more about whether study abroad students are developing intellectually, and if any particular aspects of study abroad programs are associated with this development.

Research on the psychological impact of international experiences has led some researchers to conclude that "meaning disruptions" (McNamee & Faulkner, 2001, p. 73) and restorations are a part of the international exchange experience (McNamee & Faulkner, 2001), and that culture shock (Oberg, 1960), a reaction often associated with negative stress, strain, unfamiliarity, and trauma, can be positive if it leads to personal growth (Furnham & Bochner, 1986).

For study abroad professionals, who commonly refer to the "eye-opening" changes that we see in our returning students, including students having a "different perspective" or perhaps being "more mature," having greater insight into how the experience affects our students in ways that we can measure and document would benefit our practice. As one veteran study abroad administrator commented for this book about his 27 years of experience working with study abroad students:

> They acquire a new sense of themselves and bring that sense home with them. In the midst of so many people back home who do not care or understand, students find a few who do—including us, of course, and some faculty, and increasingly, one or more gatekeepers to career opportunities. Like the Road Less Traveled, the study abroad experience makes all the difference as it continues to affect students' lives far into their adulthood.

Purpose of the Study

This study focused on one semester's study abroad student populations at eight U.S. colleges and universities. These students all studied abroad during the spring 2004 semester through the programs administered by these colleges and universities. Survey data and essays were used to assess student participation and gains in intellectual development. The purposes of this study were to determine whether gains in intellectual development occurred in students during one semester of study abroad participation, and to identify which variables (demographic variables and/or survey items) were associated with any gains in intellectual development seen in the students.

Study Variables

I chose the following study variables because of their importance in study abroad research (Engle & Engle, 2003) and higher education research, as explained later. Survey questions designed to obtain information from students on these questions will be covered in chapter 3.

Gender

The question of gender is important, for several reasons. First, study abroad participation is not proportionally even between genders. Study abroad students are and have been mostly women, consistently comprising over 60% of annual study abroad participation (IIE, 2003), what Hoffa calls the historical "gender demarcation" (Hoffa, 2007, p. 83) of studying abroad. Women comprise 56% of undergraduate students overall in the United States (Horn, Peter, & Rooney, 2000). Second, and more important, the leading researchers in this field have shown that patterns in intellectual development can be gender related. For example, intellectual developmental patterns used more often by women students tend to value their own, and others', personal experiences during the learning process (Baxter Magolda, 1992). Whereas patterns used more often by male students are typically associated with students' own learning and forming their own opinions, those more often used by women incorporate the opinions of classmates and others in their lives. Intellectual developmental patterns more often used by men also are more typically associated with reluctance to let go of certainty, and with being more threatened by the inclusion of others' ideas into their own (Baxter Magolda, 1992). Further, women tend to value educational lessons that grow out of personal relationships, such as with peers, friends, and teachers, as well as life crises and interactions with their community over traditional academic work and pedagogical techniques (Belenky, Clinchy, Goldberger, & Tarule, 1986).

The research of Baxter Magolda and Belenky, Clinchy, Goldberger, and Tarule suggests that the intense and often unfamiliar cultural interactions that characterize studying abroad, as well as the personal relationships formed with peers and teachers from other schools and possibly the host country, could be an integral part of the intellectual developmental process for some study abroad students. The "rebuilding and self-examination" (Baxter Magolda, 1992, p. 330) that can occur when studying abroad seem especially important for women's more personalized and contextualized ways of knowing. Also, what limited research there is on this subject has shown that female and male students experience studying abroad differently, particularly that women express more predeparture concerns about housing, meeting people, and dealing with unfamiliar situations (Martin & Rohrlich, 1991), and women study abroad students sometimes find the host country not as welcoming (Anderson, 2003). These concerns do not reduce their numbers since, as stated earlier, women far outnumber men in study abroad programs. However, this research suggests that women may be more aware of the challenges they are going to face when studying abroad, and possibly that many men would rather not experience that challenge, or perhaps do not initially consider studying abroad as challenging as women do. Since making meaning out of complex and challenging experiences is associated with intellectual development, the impact of gender on intellectual development when studying abroad was investigated.

Language of the Study Abroad Country

The language of the study abroad country is important because, from the standpoint of challenge and support, it is very challenging to study and live in a country whose dominant language is not one's own (Citron, 1996; Rivers, 1998; Thot, 1998). Also, the language of the study abroad country is considered an important distinguishing characteristic of study abroad program types (Engle & Engle, 2003). If supported properly, this could be the type of challenging and diverse experience that has been shown to be associated with student development in general (Pascarella, Palmer, Moye, & Pierson, 2001). The two dominant English-speaking study abroad destinations (the United Kingdom and Australia) alone account for approximately 25% of all study abroad participation annually. The other top destinations for U.S. study abroad students (Spain, France, Italy, and Mexico) are all foreign language environments. No other country besides the six mentioned receives more than 3% of the total annual study abroad student population (IIE, 2003). Since U.S. students are a reflection of their own generally monolingual society (NAFSA, 2003; Thot, 1998), the degree of challenge for students traveling to foreign language destinations could be higher than for those traveling to English language destinations, resulting in the potential for greater intellectual developmental gain. Through this study I sought to learn whether there was any evidence that this was so.

Amount of Cultural Immersion

The amount of cultural immersion built into the program is important, because it is considered by study abroad professionals an important distinguishing characteristic of study abroad program types (Engle & Engle, 2003), and because study abroad program structures historically have had different amounts of emphasis on host culture immersion experiences for students (Walker, 1999). By cultural immersion in studying abroad I mean that there are distinctions in program design and structure that directly impact the amount of time and involvement that students have with the host country culture. Two important aspects of study abroad program structure, among others, can be used to demonstrate these distinctions: (1) Where, and with whom, do U.S. students study while abroad? (2) Where, and with whom, do U.S. students live while abroad? Study abroad professionals consider both of these characteristics important ways to characterize the nature and quality of study abroad program types (Engle & Engle, 2003). In addition, examining which activities students choose to engage in while abroad also may help answer the question of whether or not cultural immersion impacts student development. These three possible factors contributing to cultural immersion while abroad are discussed next.

Where, and with Whom, Do U.S. Students Study While Abroad?

First, regarding where, and with whom, U.S. students study while abroad, the two most common program models in study abroad programs today are the direct placement experience (in which a student is placed into a host university, usually taking the same curriculum as host country students alongside host country students) and the study center (or island program) model (in which U.S. students study alongside mostly, or only, other American students, often taking courses specially designed for U.S. study abroad students) (Monalco, 2002). The direct placement experience is typically associated with greater challenge and involvement (Citron, 1996; Thot, 1998). Previous higher education research (Astin, 1984; Kuh, 1995) has shown that student involvement, particularly the amount of effort the student puts forth in the learning process, is important to student development. In this study I sought to learn whether there was any evidence that intellectual developmental gains for study abroad students in direct placement programs at foreign universities differed from those attending U.S.-dominated study centers.

Where, and with Whom, Do U.S. Students Live While Abroad?

Second, regarding where, and with whom, U.S. students live while abroad, previous research (Monalco, 2002) has distinguished study abroad student accommodation options into categories that reflect greater amounts of cultural immersion. Namely, living with a foreign host family, as opposed to living only with other U.S. students, has been positively associated with cultural immersion. Further, having host country roommates in a residence hall or an apartment could contribute to greater cultural immersion. In this study I sought to learn whether there was any evidence that intellectual developmental gains for study abroad students experiencing greater cultural immersion in their living arrangements could be found.

Students' Activities When Studying Abroad

Lastly, study abroad students can engage in activities while abroad that expose them to greater cultural immersion. As with on-campus students, the amount of effort and time put forth in these endeavors could positively affect their development. Examples of these activities include internships, student teaching, community service and volunteer work, residence life, class projects focused on the host country, quality interactions with host country faculty, clubs and activities, and serious discussions with students or others from the host country. Higher education researchers and policy makers have identified these kinds of activities as being valuable, providing opportunities to synthesize, integrate, and apply knowledge, resulting in deeper, more meaningful learning (National Survey of Student Engagement, 2000). In this study I sought to learn whether participating in activities such as those just mentioned positively contributed to gains in intellectual development.

Previous International Travel Experience

Previous international travel experience is an important variable, because research has shown that international influences on students, such as travel and having parents who are internationally mobile, can lead to greater acceptance of other cultures, greater independence, and greater international awareness compared to students who do not have such an internationally oriented upbringing (Gerner, Perry, Moselle, & Archbold, 1992). Also, college students' perceived intercultural competence is higher for those who previously had been abroad than for those who had either never been abroad or who had been abroad for a relatively short time (Martin, 1987). This study sought to examine whether there was any evidence that gains in intellectual development that may occur when studying abroad differ for those who had had a meaningful international experience prior to studying abroad and for those who had not.

My Role as Researcher

I approached this research study mainly from the role of a study abroad practitioner. Practitioners have long believed in the benefits of studying abroad, and this study was an attempt to contribute to our understanding of the topic. I approached the subject less as a theorist or methodologist and more as a curious practitioner seeking to answer some questions that may help us do our work in a better, more informed way.

I approached the subject of intellectual development on studying abroad as both a former study abroad participant and now as a study abroad professional. I studied in Madrid, Spain, in 1990–1991. My study abroad program was for two semesters, during which I was enrolled in a study center for U.S. students, worked as an English teacher, lived with a host family, and studied in a foreign language country. Prior to studying abroad, I had never been abroad (other than very short trips to Canada).

My current professional work is in study abroad administration at the State University of New York at Oswego, where I am employed as the director of International Education and Programs. I work in the daily management of study abroad programs, from recruiting and advising to program management overseas. Our college's portfolio of programs includes study centers and direct immersion programs and short-term and semester programs, with a range of housing arrangements, in both English and non-English-speaking countries.

My background in study abroad programs as both a student and a practitioner has led me to reflect on my own life experiences and how I changed as a result of studying abroad. It also has led me to ask questions about my work, in particular, the effect that studying abroad, in its variations and diversity, is having on my students currently. I sought to answer some of these questions with this research study.

CHAPTER 2

Student Development on Study Abroad

> By whatever means it is discovered, the bridge to the new world of comparative thought lies in the distinction between *an* opinion (however well "expressed") and a *supported* opinion.
>
> —William G. Perry, *Forms of Intellectual and Ethical Development in the College Years*

This chapter provides a review of studying abroad as an educational program, a review of cognitive development theories, and a review of research on the impact of studying abroad on U.S. college students. Some of the literature discusses the knowledge and linguistic gains from studying abroad, as well as developmental, or related, gains that students realize. A review of the literature on cross-cultural communication and the outcomes of international students who cross cultures also provides a context for the impact that studying abroad may have on U.S. students. A common theme running through all of the literature cited is the importance of program structure and student experience to the outcomes being studied. An attempt will be made to relate the studies described in this chapter to the broader context of student achievement when studying abroad, and on intellectual development in particular, with quotes from participating students provided to bring to life the theories and concepts presented.

Studying Abroad

Studying abroad is an academic experience, whether short term (as short as 1 week) or extended (up to a full academic year), during which students physically leave the United States to engage in college study, interaction, and more in the host country. Studying abroad may include foreign language study, residing with a foreign host family, work, and service.

Study abroad programs historically have been designed and delivered differently from one another (Citron, 1996; Engle & Engle, 2003; Walker, 1999). Programs can range from 1-week intensive study tours to 1-year immersion experiences. Students can attend university study centers taking courses abroad that are nearly identical to on-campus offerings, while other students attend a foreign university for a period of time, completely immersing themselves in the host culture (Citron, 1996; Engle & Engle, 2003; Walker, 1999). Some students will spend time almost entirely with their U.S. friends, while others, by choice or necessity, will integrate more with the host culture. Studying abroad, and its impact on student development, is an area where some meaningful, but limited, research exists, a summary of which is presented in this chapter. Research on the impact of studying abroad on intellectual, or cognitive, development is quite limited.

Cognitive Development Theory

Cognitive development theories stress the individual's information processing capacity toward the end of making meaning out of experience. Interacting with the environment, people make changes in thought processes to allow for increasingly complex ways of understanding and interpretation. This is not necessarily a smooth or an assured process of inputs to outputs, however. The tendency toward assimilation, which is the act of interpreting new experiences through existing ways of understanding, can prevent a student from more complex ways of understanding. Accommodation, on the other hand, is the ability to modify ways of making meaning to deal with complex new experiences, moving the individual to higher, more complex ways of understanding his or her experiences.

For study abroad students, the struggle to make meaning out of the vastly different experiences they are facing, at least when compared to on-campus experiences, could be viewed as an attempt at accommodation and a new developmental state. As one study abroad student described:

When I arrived in Mexico . . . I felt as if I had splashed and thrashed my way across the Rio Grande, sometimes swimming and sometimes nearly drowning . . . when I returned from my studies, I felt I had built a slender, but safe bridge between two cultures. (Miller, 1993, p. 9)

The struggle and challenge embedded in this student's words convey the anxiety and the opportunity as a student moves toward accommodation and a new level of cognitive development. It also provides a glimpse into an often-enhanced sense of individual accomplishment and self-confidence resulting from the study abroad experience. Several developmental researchers have commented on the individual's progression to higher and higher levels of complexity. Two will be explored here. In particular, the work of William Perry will be discussed and possibly introduced to the reader. Perry developed a model for understanding college student intellectual development in the 1960s, and his work holds surprising and interesting applications for today's study abroad population.

A New Look at William Perry's
Theory of Intellectual Development

Perry's *Forms of Intellectual and Ethical Development in the College Years* (1968) was based on his counseling work with Harvard University undergraduate students who, Perry observed, were at different ability levels in their understanding of the relativistic nature of their academic work. The intellectual and social atmosphere of the pluralistic university, Perry observed, was joyful and liberating to some students, while shocking and unintelligible to others. Perry sought to understand how students developed more relativistic intellectual structures during their college years, and this work led to his model of intellectual and ethical development that is still in use today.

Perry divided intellectual development into a nine-position sequence, with discernable categories. His first positions represent *dualism.* Students who view the world dualistically tend to see the world as being composed of right and wrong answers and good and bad ways of doing things, with authority figures also either right or wrong, good or bad. Alternative perspectives or considerations are not part of a dualistic student's frame of mind, nor will a student seek these alternative viewpoints (King, 1978; Perry, 1968). To this student a professor's role is to validate right and wrong information and give the student the correct knowledge.

A student participating in my study, when asked prior to her study abroad program in England what her ideal class would be like, indicated a strong preference for the type of professor often associated with this Perry position:

> The teacher would be an expert . . . brilliant, perceptive, outgoing, comfortable in their own skin, supportive, and seasoned in their field. This is an ideal teacher because they've experienced so much and have no hang-ups in regards to transferring their knowledge to others.

Rather than seeking a class atmosphere that values multiple viewpoints and a professor who encourages students to think through their own understanding of the knowledge presented, this student seemed to prefer that the professor simply transfer knowledge as is, based on the professor's (not the students') experience.

Perry's next positions are called *multiplicity*, because students at this level are able to see and appreciate that there are multiple perspectives and opinions in the world, and that individuals have the right to their own opinions. Authorities that used to provide correct answers are now suspect for providing the "right" answer, or for criticizing a student's attempt at forming an opinion (King, 1978; Perry, 1968). For multiplicity students, the study abroad program, in that it involves foreign experiences and unfamiliar ways of behaving and thinking, can provide both confirmation that there are no absolutes in the world and the opportunity to begin the process of recognizing the importance of context. "When in Rome, do as the Romans do" becomes not an abstract concept but an insight into different ways people organize their societies, maintain relationships, and, most importantly for this study, form knowledge and opinions, depending on the context.

A student in my study, reflecting back on her study abroad semester directly placed in a university in South Africa, showed evidence of new appreciation for professors who do not provide *the* right answers with the expectation that students will simply absorb and regurgitate them:

> All classes were very experiential in that it either involved direct conversation and questioning of theoretical material, or in that there were practical elements to the classroom material . . . I discovered that I really thrive off of discussion-oriented class environments. My initial reaction to the university was that the classrooms were small and overcrowded, and that the teachers were too disorganized.

Rather than judging negatively the apparent disorganization of the discussion-oriented class, this student learned that this setting is where theories get tested and assumptions are challenged. It also reinforced the new role that professors have, less focused on knowledge transfer and more focused on eliciting multiple perspectives and opinions.

Students at Perry's next positions, called *relativism*, have learned to appreciate that there are multiple perspectives and opinions, and they now understand that what is right and wrong or correct or incorrect in a given situation depends on the context. There is a larger whole to consider now, one that, as it becomes more recognizable, provides many understandable perspectives and justifiable opinions (King, 1978; Perry, 1968). Study abroad is an especially challenging and eye-opening experience that can expose U.S. students to how other societies and cultures are organized and how they function. Accommodation toward new, more flexible, and relativistic structures for interpreting the world is one possible outcome of the study abroad programs explored in this study. Choosing which course of action is appropriate in a given context remains a challenge for relativistic students, making Perry's next positions, *commitment in relativism*, still elusive for most students participating in study abroad programs and for most college students in general.

A student in my study, comparing the British and U.S. education systems at the end of her semester abroad, commented:

The style of learning in England is very different from what I was used to in America. There is a lot of emphasis on independence and self-reliance; students are expected to think for themselves and find their own answers for questions. Lecturers were there to present concepts and discuss practical applications, not to spoon-feed information to their pupils.

I spent a lot less time in class, and a lot more time in the library, researching topics and preparing for the next class. I found that I am able to think more clearly and work better under these circumstances. . . . My experience in England showed me that there are places where education is more than learning to parrot back the right opinions at the right times. It's about making your own way in the world.

This student, who presumably did not know about Perry's model, indicates quite starkly how much she prefers the ability to combine the information shared in class with her own knowledge pursuits in the library and elsewhere. Thinking for herself and not being "spoon-fed" are now vitally important to her. It should be noted that this style of teaching is not unique to England, of course, but her own understanding of its value is now evident, and it is possible that the study abroad experience contributed to that new understanding.

Perry did not research study abroad students in particular. He researched how students view knowledge in general, the role of authorities (particularly professors) in providing and validating that knowledge, the emergence within the student of a recognition that all knowledge and facts are within a context, and how eventually some decision or commitment is made based on the knowledge at hand with an understanding of its context. Further, Perry believed, like other stage theorists, that this development was irreversible. In fact, he used the term *development* not to suggest that students' later views were "better or more true" (Perry, 1968, p. 3) but rather that students' later assumptions followed, in a coherent way, patterns of increasing understanding of, and comfort with, intellectual complexity. This cannot, Perry believed, occur in reverse order; in other words, we build our intellectual capacity step by step.

Perry believed that the mind goes through "differentiations and reorganizations required for the meaningful interpretation of increasingly complex experience" (Perry, 1968, p. 4), and that eventually the mind has the "power to make meaning in successive confrontations with diversity" (Perry, 1968, p. 4). This "meaning-making" ability is the essence of intellectual development, and Perry maintained that exposure to diverse experiences and complex and challenging stimuli causes that upward developmental motion, and that once done, it is not reversible. Piaget's influence is evident here, namely, that the brain, like any muscle or organism, at first resists but then accommodates new and challenging influences on it, and once done it is stronger and more adaptable (Piaget, 1965).

King (1990) cited that one goal of higher education is for researchers and practitioners to identify types of experiences that are associated with student development. This research study seeks to determine whether studying abroad is an example of a college program that facilitates intellectual development along the Perry model.

Baxter Magolda's Model

Marcia Baxter Magolda (1992) provided an alternative model for college student development with similarities to Perry's. Her epistemological reflection model held that students in the earliest stages of development engage in *absolute knowing*, where knowledge is certain and absolute, professors possess it, and the student's role is to obtain it. *Transitional knowing* students have developed to the next stage where they know that knowledge is partially certain and partially uncertain, and the role of students is to try to understand what is coming at them, either through logic and reason or through a connection to their own experience (Baxter Magolda, 1992).

Students' growth to the *independent knowing* stage, in which they develop the confidence to listen to their voice, think for themselves, and not be bound to authority figures' determination of what knowledge is, leads to the view that knowledge is mostly uncertain. *Contextual knowing*, Baxter Magolda's last stage, is one in which students begin to make critical judgments about what to believe, based on the context of the situation. Problems and issues are now thought through, not just discussed, in order to come to some conclusion. Knowledge is still uncertain, but expertise is now recognized, leading students to accept some opinions and ideas over others (Baxter Magolda, 1992).

In her research, Baxter Magolda found that students at the transitional and independent knowing stages benefited from study abroad and international experiences. Students spoke of their increasing awareness of diversity and multiculturalism while also recognizing certain interdependencies. Interactions with complex and foreign situations through study abroad programs contributed to students placing value on their own experience, thereby lessening that of authority figures. Baxter Magolda found that development toward independent knowing seems particularly enhanced when studying abroad, in that successfully going abroad, often in a foreign language environment, led students to increasingly trust their own judgment. Gains in cultural awareness, appreciation of diversity, and insight into racial identity seemed to flow from the increased self-awareness and self-confidence as a result of studying abroad (Baxter Magolda, 1992).

It should be noted that Baxter Magolda's research design was longitudinal and traced the development of participating students throughout the college experience. Starting in the students' first semester of college and continuing past graduation, she was able to ensure that the students' entire experience was reflected in her findings.

Review of Cross-cultural Research

Some important research exists on cross-cultural experiences and intercultural communication, much of it focusing on the concept of culture shock and on foreign students studying in the United States. A brief review is presented next.

Culture Shock

The term *culture shock* was first used by Oberg in the 1950s to describe the profound anxiety and disorientation that travelers to other countries face as the familiar signs and symbols of their daily lives disappear (Oberg, 1960). Pedersen built on that concept by connecting culture shock to the formation of new developmental perspectives on the self, on others, and on the environment in order to fit in with the new culture, eventually resulting in a more culturally contextual understanding of life (Pedersen, 1995).

Bochner (1982) proposed a social-psychological model to understand culture shock, believing that people experiencing culture shock are actually in the process of reordering their cognitive structures, in effect, forming a different person. Bochner rejected as chauvinistic terms such as *adjustment* and *adaptation*, instead believing that successful travelers acquire necessary cultural skills in order to succeed in their new environment. In the process they become different, more complex people (Bochner, 1982). Bochner's model is important for the field of study abroad research because it rejects the notion that adjustments in behaviors equal a successful international experience. Students who go abroad and merely adjust or adapt to their environments might never truly understand the culture in which they are immersed. Learning about culture is different than reacting and adjusting to it. It should be noted that some college-age students going abroad for the first time may only be able to adjust, while some others are not able to do even that.

Culture shock as a psychological concept is important to study abroad research, particularly as it relates to student development theory. The experience of disequilibrium necessary for development can be viewed, in the context of international travel, as being found within the culture shock experience. Much like meeting a U.S. student of a different race or from a different region of the country can be a challenging, developmentally impactful experience for undergraduates, removing the commonality of U.S. culture also could be challenging and developmentally impactful. However, as I show from a review of study abroad research, that outcome is not guaranteed.

International Students in the United States

Before examining research on studying abroad by U.S. students overseas, a brief review of one research study conducted on international students in the United States is covered because it shows what can happen when students cross borders for academic study. Hull

(1978) found that foreign students in the United States experience loneliness, homesickness, anxiety, and general difficulties coping with their new educational environment. He found that the more interaction with local students, faculty, and others that foreign students had, the better able they were to cope with the experiences of studying abroad but also the more satisfied they were with their time there (Hull's *modified cultural contact hypothesis*). Hull found generally that, as a result of their international experiences, foreign students reported changes to their own intellectual abilities, political opinions, religious attitudes, feelings of self-confidence, and feelings of independence (Hull, 1978).

Taken together, Hull's findings shed light on what can happen when a student studies in another country. Clearly, some students have more difficulty than others trying to fit into their new culture, but all seem to experience some change from the experience, in varying degrees. Hull also showed that the amount of interaction with the host culture plays an important role in cultural learning, as well as overall satisfaction with the experience. Similar findings from studies on U.S. students abroad are discussed later.

Research on U.S. Students Studying Abroad

Studying abroad as a college program is an area where some meaningful, but limited, research has been published. While the particular focus on intellectual development along the Perry model has not been published in this way, studying abroad as a program that facilitates language acquisition, cultural learning, and gains in functional international knowledge has been researched. Research also exists that examines students' predeparture concerns and characteristics, motivations for studying abroad, and different study abroad program types. The next section presents some important research studies focusing on studying abroad.

Study Abroad Evaluation Project

One of the most comprehensive studies of the impact that studying abroad has on U.S. college students was the Study Abroad Evaluation Project (SAEP), begun in 1982 (Carlson, Burn, Useem, & Yachimowicz, 1990). The SAEP researchers compared students going abroad with those who did not, compared the impact of the host country on study abroad achievement, and also examined the impact of different student experiences when studying abroad. The study included approximately 250 students from the University of California (Berkeley, Los Angeles, and Santa Barbara campuses), the University of Colorado at Boulder, the University of Massachusetts at Amherst, and Kalamazoo College who studied abroad for their junior year, beginning in the fall of 1984. All study abroad students were studying in direct immersion programs at foreign universities, not study abroad centers with only U.S. students. Questionnaires were administered to students, both those studying abroad and a comparison group, at the end of their sophomore year and at the beginning of their senior year. The study abroad destinations were all Western European countries: France, Germany, the UK, and Sweden (Carlson et al., 1990).

Carlson et al. used several scales to measure student achievement while abroad, including international understanding, clarification of professional goals, overall satisfaction with the junior year, language acquisition, academic learning styles and abilities, and the "personal self-efficacy scale" (1990, p. 23). The authors defined this scale as one encompassing the student's social competence, both the student's attitude toward himself or herself and attitudes about socializing with peers and constructed questions to determine growth in this scale when studying abroad. The scales that are most important to my study are the ones focused on academic learning styles and abilities and personal self-efficacy, because they most closely relate to intellectual development and to student development generally.

Building on the work of Sanford (1962) and Piaget (1965), the researchers sought to understand how much the study abroad experience upset students' existing equilibria, requiring fresh adaptation toward a higher developmental level. The SAEP findings did not support the hypothesis that a study abroad experience resulted in higher levels of self-confidence and sociability, compared to a group that did not go abroad (Carlson et al., 1990).

However, the study produced interesting results on the scale measuring development in ways of thinking and learning. Perry's

(1968) work on intellectual development holds that, during their college careers, students typically progress from a simple, more absolute understanding of the nature of knowledge and academic authority to a more complex and contextual understanding. While the SAEP researchers did not measure students' intellectual development along the Perry scale, they did find that participating students showed growth toward the belief that developing one's own point of view is important, and that it is important to seek an interdisciplinary approach to knowledge. Additionally, the study showed that study abroad students returned home with a reduced emphasis on learning facts, less emphasis on grades, and a lower tendency to regard the professor as the main source of information (Carlson et al., 1990).

These findings, as related to Perry, suggest that study abroad students show a reduced tendency toward dualistic thinking and the related belief that there are absolute right and wrong answers, good and bad information, as well as sources thereof. Instead, these results suggest that some study abroad students might be moving up the Perry scale toward greater understanding of complexity (multiplicity and relativism).

Fully 100% of the SAEP study abroad students completed the bachelor's degrees, as reported in a postgraduation survey. Many also had continued on to postgraduate work (Carlson et al., 1990). However, that the study abroad students were all juniors is important to consider here, since the greatest danger of dropout occurs during the freshman year (Tinto, 1987). Of the SAEP study group, by the junior year it is likely that those who were at risk of leaving had already done so.

The study abroad students also were, on average, more satisfied with their junior year than the comparison group. As a whole, the study abroad group felt that the year abroad enriched them culturally, linguistically, academically, and personally. The perspectives students gained on the United States, the world, and on themselves were considered useful to their future lives and careers (Carlson et al., 1990). A limitation of this finding is that the full year immersion program taken by the SAEP students was the only program model studied. The study does not show how the impact would have differed based on participation in a more limited study abroad program, such as one at a study abroad center or one of a shorter duration. Nonetheless it appears from this study that studying abroad in general is an example of the type of nontraditional academic experience positively related to persistence (Tinto, 1987), learning, and development (Astin, 1984; Kuh, 1995).

Additional Study Abroad and Related Research

Study Abroad Program Structure and Self-Selection. The effect of integration into the host culture was researched through a qualitative study conducted by Citron (1996) that focused on 16 students participating in a one-semester study abroad program in Madrid, Spain. While on the surface the program appeared to have the ingredients of a highly integrated immersion experience (students living with host families and enrolled directly at a foreign institution), the researcher found that without other key elements, namely, a full-time faculty director and a structured orientation program, the students did not immerse themselves into the local culture. Citron found that the students tended to associate with each other, eat at U.S.-style restaurants, and travel with an itinerant, almost tourist, mentality (Citron, 1996). These students did not experience classic culture shock symptoms because they apparently did not choose to rely on the authentic host culture for their daily living. Given that Madrid is a cosmopolitan Western city, like many study abroad destinations, this choice is possible.

The Citron (1996) study showed that for these students and likely many others, peer influences are critical during study abroad programs, just as they are on campus (Dey, 1997). Without an experienced faculty member or director to guide their learning, these students were influenced by the general social context in which they found themselves. Nonetheless, students did report (through interviews and personal journals) greater independence, a greater willingness to get involved with international student mentoring back on their home campus, and increased confidence (Citron, 1996). This study showed that program quality and structure are important ingredients in the assessment of program effectiveness.

Kauffmann, Martin, Weaver, and Weaver (1992) presented a model for describing the personal growth and learning that occur during the study abroad experience, and they differentiated between types of study abroad experiences. The core beliefs of Kauffmann et al. are similar to those of developmental theorists, namely, that education itself means change, not only knowledge acquisition. They argued that change occurs as a result of discontinuity and disequilibrium, the set of stimuli necessitating fresh adaptation. Further, they contended that learning is holistic, synergistic, and multifaceted. Studying abroad, as stated earlier, is typically a multifaceted, challenging learning opportunity.

Kauffmann et al. distinguished between low-quality and high-quality interaction between people and their environments. High-quality interactions produced more beneficial stimuli and increased challenges and provided greater potential for growth and development. Studying abroad, then, can be seen as an example of a high-quality person-environment interaction, with further distinction within study abroad experiences between low- and high-quality interactions (Kauffmann et al., 1992).

Kauffmann et al. presented the model that follows for student development during study abroad experiences. Borrowing from earlier works of developmental researchers, their model was targeted at the study abroad student, showing development along an autonomy continuum:

Autonomy	Belonging	Cognition/ Values	Vocation	Worldview
Level I: Other-Dependent	Conventional Diffuse	Inherited	Dualistic	Encapsulated Ethnocentrism
Level II: Inner-Group Dependent	Self-selected	Searching	Relativistic	Empathic Ethnorelativism
Level III: Inter-Dependent	Open	Owned	Commitment in Relativism	Integrated Ethnorelativism

(Kauffmann et al., 1992, p. 128)

One of the conclusions of Kauffmann et al. was that study abroad students make strides in moving toward the inner-dependence level. This can be related to movement toward independent knowing in Baxter Magolda's scheme. Kauffmann et al. further described that the lower the level of development of the student, the greater potential for positive change as a result of the study abroad experience. The authors' distinction between high- and low-quality experiences is relevant to that conclusion. For example, the authors described an other-dependent-level student, who was required by her college to perform service in a developing country in the Caribbean, as experiencing an overly challenging program, with physical hardship and safety concerns on the island. The authors argued that such an overly challenging program was not conducive to positive development (Kauffmann et al., 1992).

On this point, Kauffmann et al. stated that students already at the inner-dependent level were more ready to deal with the complex and challenging situations in which study abroad students often find themselves, but that they tended to benefit less from the experience compared to their other-dependent colleagues. Kauffmann et al. found inter-dependence elusive, no matter how far a student developed. This relates well to Perry's commitment positions and Baxter Magolda's contextual knowing in that they are developmental levels that most college students also do not reach.

Research methods were not discussed at length by Kauffmann et al., and only limited insight into the demographic composition of the students involved was provided. A greater exploration of these topics would have been welcomed, given the considerable generalization of findings offered by the authors. That said, their conclusion that students at lower developmental levels benefit more from study abroad is interesting. It compares well with the findings presented later in this work, namely, that students for whom study abroad was their first meaningful international experience tended to begin study abroad programs at a significantly lower intellectual developmental level than their peers with more international exposure, but that this gap disappeared after studying abroad.

Study abroad program structures, and the impact of these on students, can vary widely, as shown earlier. One college's struggle to link studying abroad to greater multicultural learning on campus was detailed in a 1995 Fund for the Improvement of Post Secondary Education (FIPSE) grant study (Beach, 1995). Colgate University, a highly selective, predominantly Caucasian campus in rural upstate New York, typically sent half of its students abroad for one semester. The college created a new Office of Intercultural Resources (OIR) to link purposefully study abroad activities and other campus programs focused on multicultural dialogues, workshops, and support resources. This study sought to determine whether a combination of study abroad and campus programming could increase multicultural learning. Whitt, Edison, Pascarella, Terenzini, and Nora (2001) found that intentional campus programming to enhance appreciation for diversity and multiculturalism, such as diverse living arrangements and diversity workshops, can succeed.

A closer examination of which Colgate students on the Beach (1995) research project studied abroad shed light on the question of whether study abroad could enhance multicultural learning if combined with on-campus programming. While 50% study abroad participation is noteworthy, the other half of the student body that chose not to go abroad proved hard to reach for the OIR, and those students did not change their attitudes and behaviors toward multiculturalism as measured through a quantitative survey. The students who did study abroad scored higher on multicultural tolerance even before going abroad. The study concluded that there is apparently considerable self-selection for study abroad participation, indicating that studying abroad might not be causing greater tolerance and multicultural acceptance, but rather those who already are more tolerant are the ones who choose to go abroad (Beach, 1995). Colgate's particular demographics may compound this situation in that it is a small, predominantly Caucasian campus in a rural setting, and opportunities to experience diversity on campus may be more limited than those in the study by Whitt et al. (2001). Nonetheless, the Beach (1995) study cautions study abroad researchers to not assume that study abroad students hold the same beliefs and values as those on campus who do not go abroad.

Study Abroad and Gains in Global Awareness. Sutton and Rubin (2004) found that compared to their nonstudy abroad counterparts, study abroad students showed gains in their knowledge of world geography and in functional international knowledge (that knowledge needed for navigating daily routines in new, unfamiliar settings). The researchers also found that study abroad students showed a greater knowledge of global interdependence and greater political awareness. The Sutton and Rubin study also provided some evidence that studying abroad contributed to enhanced cultural relativism and reduced ethnocentrism (Sutton & Rubin, 2004). Since Perry's (1968) model defined the movement toward relativism as evidence of a higher intellectual developmental state, it may be possible that upward movement along the Perry scheme also will be seen after studying abroad.

In a similar finding, Sharma and Mulka (1993) found that study abroad students were more likely to support internationalism, were more worldly-minded, were more culturally pluralistic, and had a greater understanding of U.S. culture than those who did not go abroad. While this research seems geared more toward the "global village" purpose for studying abroad, as defined earlier, these findings can be seen in student development terms as well. For example, the students in this study returned from study abroad experiences more culturally pluralistic and more aware of U.S. culture than before. This could imply that these students are now able to see the customs and systems in place in their home country as being one of many viable ways to organize society and not the only "right" way. In student development terms, this move toward multiplicity, and perhaps even relativism, seems enhanced by students' experiences of living and studying in an environment different than their own. The stimuli of experiencing how people in those countries live, work, and go to school and the students' opportunities to take part in that foreign lifestyle result in the kind of challenging experience that Sanford (1966) described as being necessary for development.

A study by Douglas and Jones-Rikkers (2001) revealed conclusions similar to the Sharma and Mulka study, namely, that study abroad students scored higher than nonstudy abroad students on measures of international and cultural awareness (a concept they call having a "world-minded attitude"). Further, this study showed that students who studied abroad in the Central American, Spanish-speaking country of Costa Rica scored higher on a measure of "world-mindedness" than did those studying in England. The authors suggested that study abroad students have moved beyond their "comfort zone" (Douglas & Jones-Rikkers, 2001, p. 64) by studying abroad, and that this accounts for their higher "world-mindedness" scores compared to nonstudy abroad students.

Douglas and Jones-Rikkers (2001) further suggested that students studying in England scored lower than those going to Costa Rica, because England requires a lesser degree of cross-cultural interaction. However, the authors based their findings only on post scores of returning students and a control group that did not study abroad. Self-selection biases are not accounted for, since the students choosing to go abroad (and of those going abroad, those choosing to go to Costa Rica) may have already been at a higher level of "world-mindedness" than those not going abroad (and those going to England). Pre- and post-studies on the same students have been shown as the most reliable way to account for changes in student development over time (Pascarella, 2001), but this study only examined data collected after the study abroad experience. Nonetheless, the Douglas and Jones-Rikkers study sheds light on one of the research questions of my study: Does studying abroad in a foreign language country affect students differently than those studying in English-speaking countries?

A study by Drews, Meyer, and Peregrine (1996) at Juniata College showed that study abroad students are more likely to conceptualize other national groups in personal, real ways, even if unflattering. The authors found that studying abroad did not simply produce a naïve liking of others, but rather that less stereotypical, more layered, and more complex views of others resulted. Further, the researchers concluded that this complexity of thinking applied also to cultures that were not the ones visited when studying abroad. In their study, students who had studied in England indicated a greater understanding of people in China, where they had never been. In short, their study showed a tendency for study abroad students, more so than those who did not study abroad, to personalize members of other cultures, which, in their view, interferes with the process of dehumanization and fosters a more complex understanding of the world (Drews, Meyer, & Peregrine, 1996). A greater understanding of complexity is associated with higher levels of intellectual development in the Perry scheme.

A study of U.S. college students studying in Israel in the late 1960s suggested that students studying abroad in a country during a time of crisis might not view the experience as one leading toward greater tolerance and a sense of interdependence toward all people. The researcher found that students in Israel during the Six Day War in 1967 increased their feeling of hostility toward neighboring countries engaged in war with Israel (Herman, 1970). This is clearly a crisis situation unlike most, if not all, study abroad experiences today, but it contributes to our understanding of the possible effects of study abroad on students by suggesting that studying abroad may not, in every case, be associated with greater tolerance for others and a resulting sense of interdependence. Similar to the Drews et al. (1996) study, the Herman study showed that study abroad students can develop negative, unflattering views toward other people, and it also reinforces the idea that the study abroad location and structure, as well as an analysis of what study abroad students do with their time abroad, can impact student outcomes.

Other research on studying abroad also showed student progression toward developmental complexity, particularly in gains in self-confidence, appreciation for cultural difference, tolerance for ambiguity, and open-mindedness (Hansel & Grove, 1986; Kauffmann & Kuh, 1984).

The Effect of Prior International Experience. While not focused on college students, a study of U.S. adolescent children of internationally mobile parents, such as diplomats and expatriates, showed similar evidence of developmental impact as many of the studies cited earlier (Gerner, Perry, Moselle, & Archbold, 1992). Over 1,000 students in the study rated themselves more culturally tolerant and more internationally oriented than their peers in the United States. They also demonstrated greater independence than their U.S. peers (Gerner et al., 1992). Tolerance and acceptance of different cultures and lifestyles, along with an awareness of how one's society fits into the larger world, are consistent with higher developmental levels. The authors noted that internationally mobile adolescents often attend special schools and are not otherwise integrated into the host culture, suggesting that just being abroad has some developmental impact. It should be noted that this study did not address the role that these adolescents' parents play, who also must be internationally mobile, in fostering greater tolerance and international awareness.

Predeparture Student Characteristics. One study aimed at examining study abroad student characteristics and the student experience was conducted by Martin and Rohrlich (1991). The quantitative research study investigated the relationship between concerns students had prior to their study abroad experience and certain student characteristics, including gender, age, and previous international experiences. For at least one of the characteristics, gender, the researchers found significant differences. In particular, the women students in that study tended to show greater predeparture concerns regarding housing, climate, interaction with new people/making friends, use of unfamiliar currency, adjustment to new customs, and use of local transportation (Martin & Rohrlich, 1991). There were no significant differences in other areas, including homesickness, having sufficient money, language, and course work. While only representing one group of students, and only looking at predeparture concerns, Martin and Rohrlich suggested that female students viewed their experience differently from male students in several important ways, which further suggests that studying abroad may affect different students in different ways.

Summary and Conclusion

Storti (1990) described life in the expatriate community, where little interaction with the host culture is found or sought, as "sterile and vaguely unsatisfying. There is about it the aura of missed opportunities and failure of the will" (p. 34). Research on study abroad for both U.S. and foreign students generally agrees with the notion that more interaction with the host culture leads to greater attainment during the experience and greater satisfaction (Hull, 1978; Kauffmann & Kuh, 1984).

But this is not absolutely the case, as even highly integrated study abroad programs do not necessarily produce greater gains in all areas than similar time spent on the student's home campus (Carlson et al., 1990). Further, some seemingly high-interaction study abroad programs can, upon closer inspection, be enclaves of American culture, seemingly indifferent to the fascinating environment of which they are a part (Citron, 1996). And research has shown that male and female students think about and experience study abroad differently (Martin & Rohrlich, 1991), and that students who choose to study abroad differ from those who do not (Beach, 1995; Schroth & McCormack, 2000).

Lacking from the studies cited in this chapter is a more complex recognition of how different study abroad programs can be from one another, how different the experiences within the same program can be for different students, and the different ways that study abroad experiences affect different students. This research study seeks to provide some insight into the impact that these differences might have on intellectual development. It seeks to make some meaningful contribution to our understanding of study abroad and higher education generally by furthering our knowledge of the process of intellectual development during international experiences, and which factors may contribute to such development. Much study abroad research, to date, has been on practical concerns related to overcoming the problems of cross-cultural adaptation rather than on understanding what is happening to students during the process itself (Anderson, 1995). Given the effects of student involvement and campus organizational structure on student success and retention (Tinto, 1987), it is possible that the causes of students' success, or lack thereof, abroad can be linked to the type of program they are attending, to the experiences they have while they are abroad, and to their international experiences undertaken before studying abroad. If we accept that there can be different study abroad experiences and different amounts of previous international exposure, then the effects of those differences on students warrant further scrutiny. This study is an attempt to do that, examining the area of intellectual development when studying abroad.

CHAPTER 3

Focusing on Today's Students

Practice without theory is meaningless.
Theory without practice is blind.
—Anonymous

The study I conducted was an attempt to determine whether study abroad participation positively affects the intellectual development of undergraduate students. This study also sought to determine which aspects of studying abroad, determined by several variables of importance to the study abroad and higher education communities, impact intellectual development that may occur during this time. In this section I describe the conceptual framework for the study, the procedures used, instrumentation, a detailed analysis of the study sample, and limitations relevant to the study. I offer this to readers so this study can be situated in the context in which it was conducted, and so all readers can understand in which ways this study can be relevant (or not relevant) to their own campus climates.

What is most important to keep in mind is that, like any study involving people in any setting, students taking part in a study abroad program are first and foremost human beings. Human beings are impossible to predict perfectly, and their choices and responses should be respected for what they are and mean to the participants at this time of their lives. All we can do as professionals and researchers, I believe, is observe behavioral patterns that can instruct us and make our future practice better. In that regard, much of this chapter is devoted to explaining how the students taking part in this study are, in comparison to their respective populations, representative of the larger whole. This is also difficult to ensure, but in the pages that follow I outline for the reader how the students participating in this study are similar to the overall study abroad population and to study abroad students nationwide. My hope, one that

51

I believe is shown here, is that this study is seen by the reader as one that does in fact represent the larger study abroad population nationwide in such a way that the results are as generalizable as possible to other broader settings on campuses across the country.

Conceptual Framework

A repeated measures panel study was conducted on 226 study abroad students during the spring 2004 semester. A panel study of students involves the collection of data over time from the same sample of students, a sample called the "panel" (Babbie, 1990). In this case, the data came from one-semester study abroad students surveyed before and at the end of their study abroad semester. This time frame is relevant because semester study abroad programs still represent the largest single share of undergraduate students who study abroad (IIE, 2004). The study was designed so that a pre- and post-test could be administered on as many of the same students as possible to understand what intellectual development occurs during this semester abroad. Pre- and post-studies on the same students have been shown to be the most reliable way to account for changes in student development over time (Pascarella, 2001) and are considered the most sophisticated survey design for most explanatory purposes (Babbie, 1990).

The 226 participating students included those taking the pre- and the post-surveys, those taking the pre-test but not the post-test, and students taking the post-test but not the pre-test. It is not unusual for respondents in a panel study to not respond in later waves of the data collection, what is known as "panel attrition" (Babbie, 1990). An attempt was made to analyze any pattern of difference between students taking one or both parts of the study in order both to help fill in the gaps in our understanding of who the students in the sample are and how they might differ from each other.

Demographic and study variable data were collected using a questionnaire. Variables of importance to the study, such as gender, country of study abroad, and program structure, were gathered from each participating student via this method in such a way that it was impossible for the student to submit his or her survey without also submitting answers to the study questionnaire. More information on the procedures and instruments used is given later.

Procedures

In order to attract a sufficiently large number of students to participate voluntarily in this study, I invited other study abroad programs to join the study by allowing their students to be surveyed. A list of the schools involved in the study is found in Appendix A.1; a list of Institutional Review Board (IRB) requirements and results is included in Appendix A.2; and a suggested script for other schools to use to recruit students is found in Appendix A.3.

The instrument selected for the research study was the Measure of Intellectual Development (MID). The instrument is discussed at length later in this chapter. The procedure employed was to use a standard MID essay prompt for the pre-test, and a special post-prompt (developed by the Center for the Study of Intellectual Development, a research center with a special focus on intellectual development and the MID instrument, and this researcher) for the post-test. In addition to using the MID, I collected information corresponding to the other study variables needed for this study. The MID score, particularly the change that might occur from the pre-test to post-test, was the dependent variable. The four independent variables that were studied are, as mentioned earlier in the book, important both to the field of higher education and the study abroad profession. They are gender, language of the study abroad country (English versus non-English), structure of the study abroad program (direct immersion versus study center), and previous international travel experience.

Survey Web Site

For pre- and post-survey administration I used a specially designed Web site to collect both the demographic data and the MID essays. The Web site was an essential component of the study, since I was surveying students at schools other than my own, and the post-test was sent to students while still abroad. Online data collection and course delivery are quite common today. Research on the use of the Internet and Web sites in higher education has shown that students respond no differently to online surveys than to paper-and-pencil formats used in traditional survey research, and that students who are given a confidential online survey (in which the student had to supply a name) answered no differently than those who were given an anonymous online survey (Hancock & Flowers, 2001). Further, it has been shown that a Web-based survey can be distributed to a large target population at a lower cost and more quickly than traditional paper-and-pencil surveys (Couper, 2000; Schonland & Williams, 1996). Also, research on students taking a course using computer-mediated communication for course delivery reported the same level of student satisfaction with the course and the same ability to satisfy course objectives as for those students who took the same course in a traditional classroom setting (Card & Horton, 2000).

Taken together, the research cited earlier on the use of Web surveys suggests that college students today are comfortable with online learning and the use of Web sites in general and would not view an online survey as either unusual or uncomfortable. It also shows that the responses submitted online would most likely not be different than in a traditional paper-administered format. One concern about the use of Web sites for research is the low response rate (Schaefer & Dillman, 1998; Tse, 1998).

For this particular instrument, the MID is most commonly a paper-and-pencil instrument administered in a classroom or a classroom-like setting. However, it also can be done on a take-home basis if students are instructed to spend enough time on the essay so that it can be scored properly. The MID researchers have not found it to be a problem to administer the MID outside of the classroom (Moore, 1990). A description of the Web site and survey pilot testing is included in Appendix B.

Questionnaire, Choice of Questions, and Response Options

In addition to the MID instrument, I included a brief Web questionnaire in order to gather the demographic and other information necessary to analyze the data with the independent variables identified (gender, English versus non-English-speaking country, direct immersion versus study center study abroad experience, and previous international travel experience). I designed the Web site using a commercially available product. Questions pertaining to the two variables answerable with closed-ended responses, gender and direct immersion versus study center program, were written as closed-ended questions. The advantage of closed-ended questions, which are questions in which respondents have a limited choice of answers, is that the data are more easily comparable (Babbie, 1990).

One study variable, country of study abroad, was best addressed with an open-ended question, because in this case a proper closed-ended question would have necessitated an exhaustive list of possible countries from which to choose. In the case of one study variable, previous international travel experience, students were asked a closed-ended question (yes or no) if, prior to study abroad, they had traveled outside of the United States. If yes, then students were asked in an open-ended question to indicate the length of their longest trip abroad. Other questions not directly related to the research questions were also included to provide a fuller picture of the study abroad experience for the students involved.

The pre-survey included questions unrelated to this study but of use to me as a study abroad professional, concerning students' predeparture motivations and concerns. In addition, the post-survey asked students to indicate whether they had participated in any activities from a list of possible activities while studying abroad, in an attempt to gain a fuller picture of the degree of cultural immersion undertaken by each student. While not directly linked to any of the research questions, these activities were of interest to me as a researcher and study abroad professional. The final questionnaires appear in Appendix C.

The same students were invited by e-mail to participate several weeks before their departure for study abroad programs, and again at the end of, or shortly after the end of, their study abroad semester. These students attended a variety of study abroad programs in English and non-English speaking countries and included students participating in direct exchanges at foreign universities as well as students studying abroad in U.S.-only study centers (sometimes called island programs). In a smaller, pilot research project that I undertook in preparation for this larger study, I researched students who had studied abroad in Madrid, Spain, and Hong Kong, China, during 2000–2001. The results of that study, although based on a small sample, were encouraging enough to pursue this larger study in that a significant gain was observed pre-test to post-test for some students (McKeown, 2005). A brief description of those results is included in Appendix D.

Instrumentation

A variety of approaches can be used to assess intellectual development along Perry's model. At least 12 methods have been documented (Moore, 1990). Perry's (1968) original work was conducted using unstructured interviews, a time-consuming, expensive manner in which to assess students' intellectual development. Students in my study were invited to complete the MID, developed by Lee Knefelkamp and Carol Widick, a written essay adapted from Perry's (1968) model of intellectual development. The MID is currently the most widely used method, and there is extensive research on its use (Moore, 1990). With the MID, students write an essay in response to a question having to do with classroom learning, personal decision making, career plans, or, in this case, what they think they have learned while studying abroad. Trained raters score the student essays through a process of content and style analysis, and data are reported in the form of continuous variables (Moore, 1999). The trained raters measure an individual's highest thinking ability as expressed on her or his essay and assign a score corresponding to that intellectual developmental level (Moore, 1990).

Scoring

The MID instrument is scored with a three-digit number that reflects the dominant and, if necessary, subdominant positions rated in the essay. A higher Perry score corresponds to a higher level of intellectual development; examples of students at various score levels are presented later in this chapter. The MID scoring system extends the Perry continuum from a simple 2, 3, 4, or 5 score, to a three-digit number, such as 223. In this example, the number 223 means that the student is definitely at Perry position 2 (the middle number), but is opening to position 3 (the last number). For analysis and comparison on this study, I computed this number as a continuous score of 2.33, which is the average of the three numbers. A score of 233 shows the student at position 3, but not fully a three (as indicated by the first number 2). A 333 is a solid position 3, and so on (Moore, 1999).

The scoring was conducted by an organization (the Center for the Study of Intellectual Development, or CSID) well known in the field of higher education and an expert in the study of intellectual development along the Perry model. Each MID essay was scored twice by trained CSID raters, and any disagreements between these trained raters were discussed and resolved so that I received both raters' scores and their reconciled rating. The CSID documents the results of its studies and analyzes them for interrater reliability.

Examples of Students at Perry Positions

In particular, what the raters look for is evidence of Perry positions in the words expressed by student participants. For example, a student at Perry position 2, which is the multiplicity prelegitimate position (Perry, 1968), is still basically dualistic but can now at least perceive that multiplicity exists. Multiplicity is still an alien, unreal position for these students, but they can begin to recognize it at position 2.

Perry cited a position 2 student in his own research who said that he liked a certain high school history course because in that course "the teacher would be telling you exact facts . . . I like it better when they give you something concrete, exactly what happened—not go off on a tangent" (Perry, 1968, pp. 107–108). This student seems to be able to recognize that there are facts other than "exact" or "concrete" ones, but he still seems to prefer that dualistic, right and wrong, way of presenting history. It is not clear what he means by going off on "a tangent," however, his words suggest that the student can recognize that professors sometimes bring other relevant ideas and events into discussions.

The student does not like when this happens, though, and he says so in his reply. This student's response about his college class is consistent with the Perry position 2 study abroad student quoted earlier in this book who preferred a "brilliant" professor, an "expert" who knew that the job of a professor was "transferring" knowledge to the students.

Students at Perry position 3, the multiplicity subordinate position (Perry, 1968), can now begin to recognize multiple viewpoints and some of the implications of multiplicity, but they are still not giving up entirely on the idea that there are knowledge authorities. Perry believed that position 3 students' trust in these academic authorities is not threatened.

A student in my study, reflecting on her semester in London, said that she took "a Middle East class with a very knowledgeable professor. All the students in the class had their own ideas, we had people from all over the world in that class. I have learned that it is okay to tell people your ideas because they are more than willing to discuss their own and yours." This student seems to understand what multiplicity is and that it might help her learn more about the topic, but she still phrases this process with the professor's role clearly and importantly situated. Her trust in the professor's knowledge is prominently mentioned, followed by her recognition of others', and her own, ideas.

As students climb higher in position they develop through multiplicity toward more relativistic stages. Students at Perry position 4, the relativism subordinate position (Perry, 1968), now accept multiplicity. This means that multiple views are accepted as part of any discussion; that anyone has a right to an opinion, and that absolute statements are doubted with authorities being viewed more suspiciously for trying to impose them. Further, relativism is now perceived. From my research study, a student approaching this position and reflecting on his semester in Madrid wrote:

> The Spanish people who I met understood a clear division between the government and the people. When our government, and even those critical of the government, try to rile us by saying "they hate us," I know it is now true. First of all, who are "we"? Do I really have to respond to a semblance of national identity? I felt much more comfortable living in Spain than I do in the United States sociopolitically, so why can't I consider myself Spanish?

This student seems to be aware of the multiple views around him, whether in class or on the streets of Madrid, and he is comfortable with that. Further, he seems to believe that the government's authority to tell people what to do and how to think is different than what people themselves decide to do and think, and also that a concept such as "national identity" can be influenced by the context of a situation. He might not have known until living abroad that one's national identity can be shaped by where one is, evidence of a more relativistic view of that concept.

Instrument Administration Procedures

The pre-essay was administered before the students left the United States. The post-essay was administered during a period of just before to several weeks after their return. For all students, the MID pre-question was this:

> Describe a course that would represent the ideal learning environment for you. Please be as specific and concrete as possible about what this course would include; we want you to go into as much detail as you think is necessary to present clearly this ideal situation. For example, you might want to discuss what the content or subject matter would be, the evaluation procedures that would be used, the demands on you as a student, what the teacher/s would be like, and so on. Please include your explanations for why the specific course aspects you discuss are "ideal" for you.

The post-question for all students was this:

> Thank you for participating in this research project. This is NOT a program evaluation of your study abroad program.
>   Look back on your experiences in the study abroad program and reflect on your discoveries about yourself as a learner. Please be as specific and concrete as possible about what stood out for you about this program: we want you to go into as much detail as you think is necessary to give us a clear idea of your learning in the study abroad program. For example, you might want to discuss any

or all of the following topics: the content/subject matter, the kinds of teachers and teaching you experienced, the classroom atmosphere, and/or the evaluation procedures that were used. Through these experiences, what have you learned about yourself as a learner?

The pre-question is a standard MID essay prompt. The post-question was developed by this researcher specifically for study abroad research in consultation with the CSID, trained raters in scoring the MID, and was tested during a pilot study.

The MID is a production task in which students respond to an essay prompt. For production tasks, inter-rater reliability and the validity of the rating inferences are very important. The CSID recommends that two raters review each essay. Research on the MID's inter-rater reliability has demonstrated that over 93% of ratings were within one third of a position (Moore, 1990). The instrument's validity as a sound method for measuring intellectual development also has been shown to be strong. Studies comparing the MID score with intellectual measures other than those measuring the Perry scheme, such as moral judgment, report positive correlations of .45 and higher. Other studies show that MID scores move after deliberate treatments and are reasonably sensitive to change even over a relatively short time period (Moore, 1990). The majority of MID data have been collected from traditional-age college students ages 18 to 21, and studies show no consistent gender bias (Moore, 1990). For these reasons, the MID was chosen as an appropriate way to measure intellectual development in this survey of college students. It should be noted that, as with all production tasks, students' ability to convey their complex views in words is sometimes difficult, especially if the topics were new (King, 1990).

This was a confidential, not an anonymous, survey. Students were asked to include their names because many State University of New York (SUNY) students study abroad through other SUNY schools. There was, therefore, the chance that a student would be contacted both by the SUNY administering campus as well as his or her home campus. However, when the MID essays were scored, the raters did not have access to names or demographic information. Response rates for confidential surveys are typically the same as for anonymous surveys, since if a respondent does not trust the researcher enough to reply confidentially, then it is unlikely that he or she would do so anonymously either.

Sample

Study abroad students going abroad for the spring 2004 semester through eight different college-based study abroad departments were invited to participate in this research study. Participation was completely voluntary. Students typically taking the MID for research purposes over one semester, as compiled by the CSID (W. S. Moore, personal communication, October 1, 2005), often have included first-year students in deliberate programs such as orientation courses, career development classes, seminars, freshmen thinking courses, and freshmen core courses.

Besides the approximately 142 students studying abroad on programs managed by this researcher (of whom 37 participated for a response rate of 26.1%), potentially over 1,800 students were invited to participate by their respective study abroad program administrators. All of my colleagues at the other study abroad departments preferred that they contact their students directly regarding participation in the study. For this reason, I cannot be certain how many students received invitations to participate in the study. In several departments' cases, it is possible that few of the students studying abroad through the department received invitations, based on response rates from those departments' students, as well as inconsistent communication from the departmental representative to the researcher. For these reasons, I cannot state with certainty the number of students invited to participate in this study, which is a limitation.

I *can* state with reasonable certainty the number of students studying abroad through the participating schools' study abroad departments and the gender proportions of participants based on information provided by the departments directly, as well as SUNY (2004) records. Spring 2004 semester study abroad enrollment at the eight participating schools was 1,868 students. Not all schools were able to provide a gender breakdown. For this reason I calculated the gender proportions based on those five schools able to provide that information. Of those able to provide gender, a total of 1,565 studied abroad on their programs and 1,077 of these were women. As a percentage, this equals 68.8% (see Table 3.1).

TABLE 3.1
Study Participation and Gender Data

	Spring 2004
Study Abroad Total	1,868
Total for Schools Providing Gender	1,565
Female Participants	1,077
% Female	68.8

Sample totals and response rates for the participating schools are presented in Table 3.2.

TABLE 3.2
Study Participation and Response Rate

Study Participants	Study Abroad Total	Response Rate
226	1,868	12.1%

Table 3.2 shows that out of 1,868 students studying abroad through the eight colleges and universities during the spring 2004 semester, 226 students participated at some point in the research study. The overall study response rate was 12.1%. The response rate from the researcher's own department's programs, where more control was exerted over procedures and communications with students, was considerably higher (26.1%) and could be considered a good response rate compared with other Web-based surveys (Van Hoof & Verbeeten, 2005) and with comparable surveys of study abroad students (Vande Berg, Balkcum, Scheid, & Whalen, 2004). As stated earlier, response rates from some participating schools were low, and the involvement of students studying abroad on those pro-

grams was difficult or impossible to determine. This same outcome has been observed in other research on study abroad students over multiple institutions (Vande Berg et al., 2004). I chose many schools with the hope that the benefit of including more schools and students in the study would outweigh the relatively poorer response rates, provided that those students were representative of the overall population of study abroad students being studied.

Subsamples: Pre and Post, Pre Only, Post Only

Tests were performed to determine whether the study sample of spring 2004 semester study abroad students was representative of the population from which it was drawn, as well as whether the subsamples were representative of the study sample. A series of chi-square tests and tests for two proportions was performed.

A total of 226 undergraduate students participated in this spring 2004 study of study abroad semester students. That total is comprised of individual students taking both pre- and post-administrations, as well as those taking pre only and post only. Table 3.3 provides a brief overview of these three groups, including gender breakdown; a more detailed analysis follows:

TABLE 3.3
Comparison of Study Sample, Study Subsamples, and Population for Gender

	Study Sample	Pre and Post	Pre Only	Post Only	Population
Overall	226	98	30	98	1,868
Female	167	72	19	76	1,077
% Female	73.9%	73.5%	63.3%	77.6%	68.8%

Note: Pre and Post = those students taking both the pre- and post-study instruments; Pre Only = those students taking the pre-instrument only; Post Only = those students taking the post-instrument only; % female of population total was determined by dividing the number of females studying abroad by the total number of students studying abroad when both figures were available; 1,077/1,565 = .688.

Table 3.4 shows the results of chi-square tests performed on the three subsamples: pre and post, pre only, and post only. The tests

The First Time Effect

were performed to determine whether the compositions of the three subsamples showed significant differences for gender, language of study abroad country, and program structure.

TABLE 3.4
Chi-Square Tests for Gender, Language, and Program Structure in Subsamples

	Gender		Language		Program Structure	
	Female	*Male*	*English*	*Non-English*	*Island*	*Immersion*
Pre and Post	72	26	44	54	53	45
Pre Only	19	11	13	17	—	—
Post Only	76	22	42	56	74	24
Chi-square	2.423		0.086		9.864	
DF	2		2		1	
N	226		226		196	
p	0.298		0.958		0.002*	

Note: Program structure information was collected on the post-survey and is unavailable for Pre Only students; Island = students studying abroad on programs with mostly or entirely U.S. students; Immersion = students studying abroad on programs with mostly or entirely host country students; dashes indicate information not collected.

*p < .05.

Gender

As shown in Table 3.4, there were three subsamples: those taking both the pre- and post-surveys, those taking the pre-survey only, and those taking the post-survey only. The chi-square test revealed that there were no significant gender differences for the three subsamples. The calculated chi-square value was 2.423 (DF = 2, N = 226), p = 0.298.

Language of Study Abroad Country

Table 3.4 shows the results of a chi-square test performed on the three subsamples (pre and post, pre only, and post only) to determine whether the compositions of the three subsamples showed significant differences based on the language of the country in which the students studied. The chi-square test revealed that, based on a sample size of 226, there were no significant differences for the three subsamples for their language of study abroad country. The calculated chi-square value was 0.086 (DF = 2, N = 226), p = 0.958.

Study Abroad Program Structure

Study abroad programs can be grouped into two broad categories as described earlier: *immersion programs*, in which a U.S. study abroad student studies mostly or entirely with students from the host country, often directly at a foreign university; and study center programs, sometimes called *island programs*, in which a U.S. study abroad student studies mostly or entirely with other U.S. students, often in a specially designed study center operated by a U.S. university or organization for U.S. students.

Table 3.4 also shows the results of a test performed to determine whether the expected outcome of respondents in the three subsamples showed significant differences based on the structure of their chosen study abroad program. For this test, pre only students could not be included because information pertaining to program structure was gathered through the post-survey. For both program structure categories, students were assigned to the group representing the participating students' own descriptions of their study environments.

As shown in Table 3.4, the chi-square test revealed significant differences for the two subsamples on program structure. The calculated chi-square value was 9.864 (DF = 1, N = 196) with the p-value significant at the .05 level (p = 0.002). This means that for the two subsamples there is a significant difference between the expected and actual outcomes for the proportion of students who study abroad on immersion programs and those taking part in U.S. study center (or island) programs.

A test for two proportions was performed to confirm the aforementioned chi-square result for program structure. The results of that test confirmed (p = 0.001) that the proportion of students taking both the pre- and post-surveys who had studied abroad on a U.S. study center program was significantly smaller than the proportion of students in the study who had taken the post-survey only. This means that students in the subsample who self-selected to take both the pre- and post-surveys in this study are not necessarily representative of the entire study sample on the variable of program structure. As will be seen later, however, this descriptive category (program structure) was not a variable impacting intellectual development on study abroad, making this discrepancy in subsamples of little importance.

Previous International Travel

Results from a chi-square test for previous international travel experience are presented next. For this test, students were asked on the accompanying survey if they had traveled internationally prior to study abroad, and if so for how long. Students were separated into three groups for purposes of analysis: (1) those indicating they had never traveled abroad before, (2) those indicating they had, and (3) of those indicating yes, those whose travel abroad was for less than 1 month. This was done so a comparison could be made to a published national study on study abroad, which will be discussed later in this chapter.

As shown in Table 3.5, of the 226 total respondents in the study sample, there were three subsamples: those taking both the pre- and post-surveys, those taking the pre-survey only, and those taking the post-survey only. This test was performed to determine whether the respondents in the three subsamples showed significant differences based on their previous international travel experience. The chi-square test revealed that, based on a sample size of 226, there were no significant differences across the three subsamples for their previous international travel experience. This proved to be the case across the three categories tested: no previous international travel, travel for less than 1 month, and travel for 1 month or longer. The calculated chi-square value was 1.143 (DF = 4, N = 226), p = 0.887. These data are presented in this way to identify students whose previous international travel was of such short duration (such as vacation travel) that it warranted separate categorizing and to be able to compare it with one published study that also researched this question. More on this comparison, and other comparisons of generalizability of the research data, will be covered in the next section.

TABLE 3.5
Chi-Square Test for Previous International Travel in Subsamples

	None	*Less Than 1 Month*	*1 Month or Longer*
Pre and Post	32	35	31
Pre Only	12	9	9
Post Only	38	33	27

Note: Chi-square value = 1.143; DF = 4; N = 226; p = 0.887.

Comparisons of Generalizability

A series of tests was performed to determine whether the respondents in the study sample were representative of the population from which they were drawn and to analyze how the sample and population both compared to relevant published studies of semester study abroad programs. Two national comparison studies were considered for comparison with the sample: the annual Open Doors (IIE, 2003) report and the Monalco (2002) study of third-party study abroad providers. The Open Doors report is one of the most comprehensive documents published in the field of international education and is widely used. It categorizes study abroad participation, among other international education data, into meaningful groupings and provides for longitudinal analysis. One drawback to the Open Doors data, however, is that it is not possible to break the data into subgroups in many cases. For example, while study abroad participation is organized into categories of duration (1 year, semester, summer, etc.) and categories of country of study abroad, it is not possible to view the data by country and duration (i.e., percentage of semester study abroad students who went to English-speaking countries), and so on. The Monalco study, published in 2002, reports on nine of the largest third-party providers of study abroad programs. This refers to those universities and other organizations that provide study abroad programs to thousands of students each year from other colleges and universities, mainly on semester programs (the focus of this research study). For that reason, the Monalco study is most useful for comparison and is cited in the pages that follow. In addition, one study (Martin & Rohrlich, 1991) is cited for comparisons on the variable of previous international travel.

Gender

The comparison results for gender are presented in Table 3.6:

TABLE 3.6
Chi-Square Test for Gender of Sample, Population,
and National Comparison Group

Group	Gender	Frequency
Study Sample	Male	59
	Female	167
Study Population	Male	488
	Female	1,077
National Comparison	Male	4,838
	Female	10,588

Note: The National Comparison Group data are from "Survey of Third Party Providers: Final Report," by Monalco, 2002, Milwaukee, WI: Monalco. Chi-square value = 2.87; DF = 2; N = 17,217; p = 0.238.

As shown in Table 3.6, the chi-square test revealed no significant gender differences for the three groups. The calculated chi-square value was 2.87 (DF = 2, N = 17,217), p = 0.238.

A test for two proportions was performed testing the proportion of females in the study sample directly against the proportion in the population; a second test was performed testing the study sample female proportion directly against a national comparison group (Monalco, 2002); a third test was performed testing the population directly with the national comparison group for proportion of females. Results are shown in Table 3.7 with p-values. These results further show that at the .05 level of significance there were no significant differences in the proportion of females in the study sample and the population from which they were drawn. The results also show that there were no

TABLE 3.7
Gender Test for Two Proportions for
Study Sample, Population, and Comparison Group

Group	Study Sample	Population	National Comparison Group
Study Sample		p = 0.107	p = 0.074
Population	p = 0.107		p = 0.883
National Comparison Data	p = 0.074	p = 0.883	

Note: Proportion of female participants was compared in each test. The National Comparison Group data are from "Survey of Third Party Providers: Final Report," by Monalco, 2002, Milwaukee, WI: Monalco.

significant differences in the proportion of women in the study sample versus a national comparison study. Finally, there were no significant differences in the proportion of women in the population versus the national comparison study. For the variable of gender, then, my study data should be viewed as being statistically comparable and generalizable to larger study abroad populations nationwide.

Language of Study Abroad Country

Generalizability comparison results for the language of the study abroad country are presented in Table 3.8. The chi-square test revealed significant differences for the three groups on the language of the study abroad country chosen by the students included in each group. The calculated chi-square value was 20.938 (DF = 2, N = 20,872), p = 0.000. This would be troubling to the study if the study sample could not be viewed as comparable and generalizable to larger populations of study abroad students nationwide on the language variable.

A follow-up test for two proportions was performed testing the proportion of students studying in English language countries (defined as those programs in Australia, England, Ireland, New Zealand, Northern Ireland, and Scotland) in the study sample directly against the proportion in the study population; a second

TABLE 3.8
Chi-Square Test for Language of Sample,
Population, and National Comparison Group

Group	Language of Study Abroad Country	Frequency
Study Sample	English	99
	Non-English	127
Study Population	English	843
	Non-English	1,014
National Comparison Group	English	7,527
	Non-English	11,262

Note: The National Comparison Group data are from "Survey of Third Party Providers: Final Report," by Monalco, 2002, Milwaukee, WI: Monalco. English language programs refer to those programs in Australia, England, Ireland, New Zealand, Northern Ireland, and Scotland. Chi-square value = 20.938; DF = 2; N = 20,872; p = 0.000.

test was performed testing the study sample proportion directly against the national comparison group (Monalco, 2002); and a third test was performed testing the population directly with the national comparison group. Results follow (see Table 3.9), with p-values shown:

TABLE 3.9
Language Test for Two Proportions for
Study Sample, Population, and Comparison Group

Group	Study Sample	Population	National Comparison Group
Study Sample		p = 0.649	p = 0.259
Population	p = 0.649		p = 0.000*
National Comparison Group	p = 0.259	p = 0.000*	

Note: The National Comparison Group data are from "Survey of Third Party Providers: Final Report," by Monalco, 2002, Milwaukee, WI: Monalco.

*p < .05.

As shown in Table 3.9, upon further analysis using the test for two proportions, the study sample proportion studying in English language countries shows no statistically significant difference with either the study population or the national comparison data. The study population proportion, while showing no statistically different results from the study sample, does show a statistical difference compared to the national comparison group. Taken together, these results suggest that at the .05 level of significance, the study sample shows no statistically significant differences with either the study population or the national comparison data, and therefore the chi-square results were influenced by the study population's relation to the national comparison data only. This is important because it then allows us to consider the study sample as statistically comparable and generalizable to larger study abroad populations for the important variable of the language of the study abroad country.

Program Structure: Immersion versus Island Program

A variable of importance to the study abroad field is the immersion program versus the U.S. study center (island) program. Data on this variable were not available from most of the colleges and universities that comprised the study population. Limited comparison data were available with the national comparison data (Monalco, 2002). A test for two proportions showed that the proportion of students in my research study, indicating that they had studied in an immersion program (35.2%), was statistically different (p = 0.009) from the proportion of those in the Monalco (2002) study (44.2%). Recall that there was a significant difference on this variable found during the analysis of the study subsamples. Therefore, it is likely that on the variable of program structure we cannot make comparisons between this study's participants and larger study abroad populations with as much confidence.

Prior International Experience

Little national data are available on prior international experiences of study abroad students. One research study that examined this facet of study abroad participants is presented in Table 3.10. Martin and Rohrlich (1991) found that in a study of 482 undergraduate study abroad students, 120 (or 24.9% of the study sample) had had no prior international travel before studying abroad. In the Martin and Rohrlich study, of those reporting that they had traveled abroad prior to studying abroad, 155 had done so for less than 1 month. Taken together, this means that 275 students, or 57.1%, of the Martin and Rohrlich study sample had either not been abroad before, or had done so for a short duration.

For my research study, I also asked students for the duration of their prior international travel, with the intent of identifying students whose previous international travel was of such short duration (such as vacation travel) that it warranted separate categorizing. Seventy-six of the 226 students in my sample, or 33.6%, reported that the study abroad experience was their first trip abroad. Of those in my study indicating that they had traveled abroad prior to studying abroad, 65 had done so for less than 1 month. Taken together, this means that 141, or 62.4%, of my study sample had either not been abroad before, or had done so for a short duration. Data from my research study and those from the Martin and Rohrlich study are presented in Table 3.10:

TABLE 3.10
Study Sample Compared with Martin and
Rohrlich Data on Prior International Travel

	Sample Size	No Travel	Less Than 1 Month	Combined
Martin and Rohrlich	482	120 (24.9%)	155 (32.2%)	275 (57.1%)
This Study	226	76 (33.6%)	65 (28.8%)	141 (62.4%)

Note: The Martin and Rohrlich data are from "The Relationship between Study-Abroad Student Expectations and Selected Student Characteristics," by J. N. Martin and B. Rohrlich, 1991, *Journal of College Student Development, 32.*

Table 3.10 shows the number and percentage of study abroad students in this study with and without prior international travel and compares that with another research study. For comparison, a test for two proportions was performed to determine whether statistically significant differences could be observed comparing these two samples. The results are presented in Table 3.11, with p-values given:

TABLE 3.11
Test for Two Proportions for Prior International Travel

	SS No Travel	SS 1 Mo	SS Combined
MR No Travel	p = 0.019*		
MR 1 Mo		p = 0.357	
MR Combined			p = 0.175

Note: SS No Travel = study sample students indicating that they had no prior international travel before studying abroad; SS 1 Mo = study sample students indicating prior international travel of less than 1 month; SS Combined = study sample students with no prior international travel combined with those traveling for less than 1 month; MR = Martin and Rohrlich study data. The Martin and Rohrlich data are from "The Relationship between Study-Abroad Student Expectations and Selected Student Characteristics," by J. N. Martin and B. Rohrlich, 1991, *Journal of College Student Development, 32.*

*$p < .05$.

The results in Table 3.11 show that the proportion of students in the Martin and Rohrlich (1991) study indicating no prior international travel was significantly lower than the proportion for this study (p = 0.019). However, when including those students whose prior international travel was less than 1 month, no significant differences between the two samples were found for either the groups indicating prior international travel of less than 1 month or the combined groups. Since no other data were available on the question of prior international experience, the Martin and Rohrlich study was used as the source of comparison data. Based on this comparison study, the study data from the study presented in this book should be viewed as comparable and generalizable with available data on this variable.

Living Arrangements Overseas

One variable of importance to the study abroad field provided little comparison data nationally: living arrangements overseas. The Monalco (2002) study, cited previously, categorized its program providers by housing type offered and found that of the nine largest third-party providers studied, 14% offered an apartment living option (either with U.S. students, with host country students, or a

TABLE 3.12
Study Abroad Participation by Country

	Participants	Percent of Total
Australia	28	12.4%
Belize	1	<1%
Brazil	1	<1%
Canada	1	<1%
China	1	<1%
Costa Rica	1	<1%
Cuba	4	1.8%
Czech Republic	2	<1%
Denmark	1	<1%
Dominican Republic	1	<1%
Egypt	1	<1%
England	56	24.8%
France	24	10.7%
Germany	1	<1%
Greece	3	1.3%
Ireland	7	3.1%
Italy	38	16.8%
Japan	3	1.3%
Mexico	5	2.2%
New Zealand	7	3.1%
Puerto Rico	2	<1%
Scotland	1	<1%
South Africa	3	1.3%
Spain	33	14.6%
The Netherlands	1	<1%
Total	226	100%

combination); 18% offered a residence hall option (either with U.S. students, with host country students, or a combination); 26% offered a host family option; and 42% offered independent living or other options (Monalco, 2002). As one element of comparison for these categories, of the 196 students taking the post-survey for my research study, 63 (32.1%) responded that they lived with a host family.

Countries of Study Abroad Participation

The 226 students who took part in this research study studied in 25 different countries. Of those 25 countries, the overwhelming proportion, 88%, studied in countries in Western Europe and Australia/New Zealand, as is typical of study abroad participation rates nationwide; the top five countries represented in my study were England, Italy, Spain, Australia, and France, which compare closely to national participation data (IIE, 2005). Table 3.12 lists the study abroad countries for the 226 students participating in this study.

CHAPTER 4

The Experience of First Time Travelers

The relationship between the individual and the environment is so extensive that it almost overstates the distinction between the two to speak of a relationship at all.

(T)he cognitive operations necessary for solving certain problems are activated in culturally specific ways. It may not be possible in a foreign culture to recognize the nature of the problem with which one is faced, or to think about the problem in the appropriate way.

—Bruce Wexler, *Brain and Culture*

The results of this research study are reported in this chapter and specifically seek to answer the questions posed in chapter 1, whether or not students participating in a one-semester study abroad program show positive gains in intellectual development, and which variables, if any, contribute to this outcome. In addition, results from this study are presented within the context of current literature on studying abroad and higher education.

Spring 2004 Study Group Descriptive Data

In chapter 3 I described the study population and sample in detail and concluded that, generally speaking, the data in this study represent well what we know about study abroad students nationally for purposes of analysis and generalizability. A brief summary of the spring 2004 study group is presented in Table 4.1.

Note that the MID instruments submitted by respondents were not always of sufficient length to be scored. For that reason, the sample sizes presented throughout this chapter may not be exactly the same as the totals presented in Table 4.1.

TABLE 4.1
Study Participants and Gender

	Study Participants	Pre and Post	Pre Only	Post Only
Female	167	72	19	76
Male	59	26	11	22
Total	226	98	30	98

Note: Pre and post = those students taking both the pre- and post-surveys; Pre only = those students taking only the pre-survey; Post only = those students taking only the post-survey.

Table 4.1 shows that of those participating in the study, 98 of the 128 students who took the pre-survey also took the post-survey (76.6%). This compares favorably to other studies of study abroad students over multiple institutions (Vande Berg et al., 2004). Of the 98 students taking both the pre- and post-MID essay instruments, 85 were of sufficient length to be scored by the raters of the CSID. Descriptive statistics for these 85 are presented in Table 4.2.

TABLE 4.2
Descriptive Statistics for Pre- and Post-Students

	n	M	SD
Pre-score	85	3.09	0.35
Post-score	85	3.09	0.29

Table 4.2 shows that of the 85 students taking both the pre- and post-surveys during this study, the mean MID score did not change.

Table 4.3 is a summary of the 85 pre- and post-students' study data.

Statistical Design

This study was a quantitative research study employing a series of paired t tests to compare means for the same (pre- and post-) students

TABLE 4.3
Pre- and Post-Students Data Summary

Code no.	Pre score	Post score	Gain	Gender (1 = f, 0 = m)	Country (0 = eng, 1 = non)	Abroad before? (0 = no, 1 = yes)	Abroad before min. 2 weeks? (0 = no, 1 = yes)	Program structure (0 = US, 1 = non)
1	2.67	3	0.33	1	1	0	0	1
2	3.33	3	−0.33	0	0	1	0	1
3	3	3.33	0.33	1	0	0	0	1
4	3	3	0	1	1	1	1	0
5	3	3	0	1	1	1	1	0
6	3.33	3	−0.33	0	1	0	0	0
7	2.67	3	0.33	1	1	1	1	1
8	3	3	0	0	0	0	0	0
9	2.67	3.67	1	1	0	0	0	1
10	3.33	2.67	−0.66	0	0	1	1	0
11	3	3.33	0.33	1	0	0	0	1
12	2.67	3	0.33	0	0	0	0	1
13	3	3	0	1	0	1	1	1
14	3	3.33	0.33	1	0	1	1	1
15	3.67	3	−0.67	1	0	1	1	0
16	3	3	0	1	1	1	1	0
17	2.67	3	0.33	1	0	0	0	1
18	3	3.33	0.33	0	1	1	0	0
19	3.33	3	−0.33	1	1	1	1	0
20	3	2.67	−0.33	1	0	0	0	1
21	3	3	0	1	0	0	0	0
22	2.67	3	0.33	0	1	1	1	1
23	3	3.33	0.33	0	1	0	0	0
24	3	3	0	1	0	0	0	1
25	3.5	3	−0.5	0	0	1	1	0
26	3.67	3	−0.67	1	1	1	0	0
27	4.33	3.67	−0.66	0	1	1	1	0
28	4.33	3.33	−1	1	0	0	0	1
29	2.5	3	0.5	0	0	1	1	0
30	3	3	0	1	0	0	0	1
31	3	2.67	−0.33	1	1	1	1	0
32	2.67	3.33	0.66	1	1	1	1	0
33	3	2.67	−0.33	1	0	0	0	1
34	3	3	0	1	1	1	1	0
35	3	3	0	1	0	1	1	0
36	2.67	3	0.33	1	1	0	0	0

(continued on next page)

TABLE 4.3 *(continued)*

Code no.	Pre score	Post score	Gain	Gender (1 = f, 0 = m)	Country (0 = eng, 1 = non)	Abroad before? (0 = no, 1 = yes)	Abroad before min. 2 weeks? (0 = no, 1 = yes)	Program structure (0 = US, 1 = non)
37	3	3.67	0.67	1	1	1	1	1
38	3.33	3.33	0	0	1	1	1	0
39	3.33	3.33	0	1	0	1	1	1
40	3.67	3.33	−0.34	1	1	1	1	0
41	3.67	3	−0.67	1	0	0	0	1
42	3.33	3.33	0	0	1	1	1	0
43	2.67	3.67	1	0	0	1	1	1
44	3.33	2.67	−0.66	1	1	1	1	0
45	3.33	3.33	0	0	0	0	0	0
46	3	2.67	−0.33	1	0	1	1	0
47	3	3	0	1	0	1	0	0
48	3	3	0	1	0	0	0	1
49	2.67	2.67	0	1	1	0	0	0
50	3	3	0	0	1	1	1	0
51	3	3	0	1	0	1	1	0
52	3	3	0	1	1	1	1	1
53	3.5	3.67	0.17	0	1	1	1	1
54	3	2.67	−0.33	1	1	1	1	0
55	2.67	3	0.33	1	1	1	1	1
56	3	3.67	0.67	1	1	1	1	1
57	2.67	3.5	0.83	1	0	0	0	0
58	3.33	3.33	0	1	0	1	1	1
59	3	3	0	1	0	1	1	1
60	3.33	3.33	0	1	1	1	1	1
61	3	3	0	1	1	1	1	0
62	2.67	2.5	−0.17	1	1	0	0	1
63	3	3.33	0.33	1	0	1	1	1
64	2.67	3	0.33	1	1	0	0	0
65	3	3	0	0	1	1	1	1
66	3	2.67	−0.33	1	1	1	1	0
67	3.33	3	−0.33	1	1	0	0	0
68	3	3	0	1	0	1	1	0
69	3.33	3.5	0.17	1	1	1	1	0
70	3.33	2.5	−0.83	1	0	1	1	0
71	2.67	3.67	1	0	1	1	1	0
72	3	3.5	0.5	1	0	1	1	1
73	3.33	3	−0.33	1	1	1	1	0
74	3.33	2.67	−0.66	1	1	1	1	0

(continued on next page)

TABLE 4.3 *(continued)*

Code no.	Pre score	Post score	Gain	Gender (1 = f, 0 = m)	Country (0 = eng, 1 = non)	Abroad before? (0 = no, 1 = yes)	Abroad before min. 2 weeks? (0 = no, 1 = yes)	Program structure (0 = US, 1 = non)
75	3	3	0	0	0	0	0	1
76	3	3	0	1	1	1	0	0
77	3	3	0	1	0	1	1	0
78	3	3	0	1	0	0	0	1
79	3.33	3.33	0	1	1	1	1	0
80	2.67	2.67	0	1	0	0	0	0
81	2.67	3.33	0.66	1	0	0	0	1
82	3.67	3.5	−0.17	0	1	1	0	0
83	3.67	3	−0.67	0	0	0	0	1
84	3.33	3	−0.33	1	0	1	1	1
85	3	3	0	1	1	1	1	1
M	3.09	3.09	0.00					
SD	0.35	0.29	0.42					
totals	85	85	85	63	43	56	50	38
% of sample				74.1%	50.6%	65.9%	58.8%	44.7%

Note: Gain = Post-score minus pre-score; Country = 0 for English-speaking study abroad destinations and 1 for foreign language destinations; Abroad before? = 0 if student had not been abroad prior to studying abroad and 1 if student had been abroad prior to studying abroad; Abroad before min. 2 weeks? = 0 if student had not been abroad for at least 2 weeks prior to studying abroad and 1 if student had been abroad for at least 2 weeks prior to studying abroad; Program structure = 0 if student studied mostly with other U.S. students and 1 if student studied mostly with non-U.S. students.

participating in study abroad programs. I used paired t tests where appropriate, because the pre-post study involved the same students. Also, I used 2–sample t tests where appropriate to make comparisons between groups (such as males and females), because those are not the same students.

Analysis Using t Tests

Analysis using t tests was performed on the data in numerous ways. First, a test was performed comparing the MID pre-score for the two groups representing students who took both the pre- and post-surveys, and all pre-. This was done to learn whether the students participating in both administrations of the study were comparable to all of those students taking the pre-portion. Next, a series of tests was performed testing whether the mean MID scores for several groups were equivalent or showed differences.

Two types of tests were performed: paired t tests and 2–sample t tests using Minitab. The paired t tests were performed on pre- and post-MID score data from the same students (pairs of students) whenever possible. However, it was not always possible to test the same students pre- to post-, therefore a series of 2–sample t tests was performed; 2–sample t tests allow us to compare the means from two samples of different sizes and characteristics, but when compared give us insight into their relationship (Aczel, 1993).

Analysis by Pre-Score

A comparison of mean pre-scores for the participating students who took both the pre- and post-surveys versus all taking the pre showed no significant difference between the two groups. The 85 taking both the pre- and the post-scored a mean 3.09 against all 120 taking the pre- who scored 3.06. No significant difference was observed between these two groups, indicating that the sample of 85 taking both the pre- and the post- was comparable to the larger study sample. Based on this result, a series of tests was performed to address the specific research questions in the study.

Research Questions

Question 1: Gains in Intellectual Development during Study Abroad

1. Did students participating in a one-semester study abroad program show gains in intellectual development?

Examining overall changes in MID scores over one semester for the study group (pre- to post-) showed no evidence that mean scores for the post-group were higher than the pre-group, for both paired sample and 2–sample tests (see Table 4.4 for those results).

TABLE 4.4
Mean Scores Pre- to Post-

	Paired			2-Sample		
	M	SD	n	M	SD	n
Pre-	3.09	0.35	85	3.06	0.37	120
Post-	3.09	0.29	85	3.06	0.33	173
p	0.97			1		

As shown in Table 4.4, the mean MID scores for the pre- and post-groups were not significantly different. This was true for both the paired sample and the 2–sample tests. This means that post-scores were not significantly higher than pre-scores. That this research study did not show significant gains in intellectual development for all students over one semester is not entirely surprising when placed in the context of existing research on college students.

Regarding research on college students generally and the MID instrument, prior studies have shown that the biggest gains in MID scores occur typically in transition points such as the first year and the latter part of senior year. The MID researchers think this is so perhaps because of targeted interventions such as freshman seminars and senior capstone courses (W. S. Moore, personal communication, April 27, 2005). In this study, of the 85 students completing both pre- and post-tests, none were first-year students. In fact, 89% (76 out of 85) were juniors or seniors, with juniors being most common. Further, there was no evidence that the study abroad semester programs included targeted interventions designed to enhance intellectual development. In addition, researchers have found that it is not unusual for majorities of study samples taking the MID instrument to show no increase in score (W. S. Moore, personal communication, October 1, 2005). On this study, 24 of the 85 students (28%) completing both the pre- and post-tests showed a gain of at least one third of a Perry position. Studies of semester-long treatments have shown that this percentage can range from 32% to 54% (W. S. Moore, personal communication, October 1, 2005). Therefore, it is not entirely surprising that, overall, the sample being studied in this research study showed no significant gains.

I sought to explore study abroad as a possible activity that, like the targeted interventions mentioned earlier, might promote intellectual development in participating students. There is no evidence from this study that this is the case for all students.

Existing research on study abroad students and the move toward study abroad program classification (Engle & Engle, 2003), combined with the recognition that program structure impacts student outcomes (Citron, 1996), and that program participant characteristics impact the student experience (Beach, 1995; Martin & Rohrlich, 1991; Schroth & McCormack, 2000), suggest that studying abroad, like all academic programs and college activities, can vary greatly by structure, degree of deliberate planning, and student participation. Much like on-campus programs, the outcome of a study abroad program likely depends on its components, its quality, and its participating students. Therefore, a more sophisticated analysis with relevant research questions and variables, as was done in this study, is a step toward forming a more complete picture of study abroad student outcomes.

Question 2: Gains in Intellectual Development during
Study Abroad for Female and Male Students

2. Did female and male students show the same patterns in their intellectual development when studying abroad?

Examining overall changes in MID scores over one semester separately for the female and male groups (pre- to post-) showed no evidence that mean scores for the post-groups were higher than the pre-groups, for both paired sample and 2–sample tests. Tables 4.5 and 4.6 show those results for both genders.

As shown in Tables 4.5 and 4.6, mean MID scores for the pre- and post-groups were not significantly different for both females and males. This was true for both the paired sample and the 2–sample tests. These results suggest that there is no evidence that either males or females show significant gains in intellectual development as measured by their MID scores during one semester of study abroad, and that there is no difference in the pattern of development between the genders.

TABLE 4.5
Female Mean MID Score Pre- to Post-

	Paired			2-Sample		
	M	SD	n	M	SD	n
Pre-	3.06	0.31	63	3.02	0.33	85
Post-	3.05	0.28	63	3.04	0.32	131
p	0.87			0.76		

TABLE 4.6
Male Mean MID Score Pre- to Post-

	Paired			2-Sample		
	M	SD	n	M	SD	n
Pre-	3.17	0.43	22	3.16	0.47	35
Post-	3.20	0.29	22	3.12	0.35	42
p	0.76			0.69		

Some research has been conducted (Anderson, 2003; Martin & Rohrlich, 1991; Medina-Lopez-Portillo, 2004) on the different experiences of men and women students during study abroad, but such differences do not seem to have led to any significant differences in intellectual development for either gender in this study. For example, Martin and Rohrlich (1991) found that women, at a statistically significant level, were more likely than men to express pre-departure concerns about studying abroad, including concerns about their housing situation, making new friends, using unfamiliar currency, using transportation while abroad, and adjusting to new customs. Anderson (2003) found that women study abroad students sometimes find the host country inhospitable during the study abroad program. Drawing upon studies done with U.S. study abroad students in Spain, Russia, and Costa Rica, Anderson concluded that women more often than men perceived their study abroad location as unwelcoming, restrictive, and at times unsafe. She noted that U.S.

females often said that they attracted unwanted attention because of their clothes and behaviors that, while culturally acceptable in the United States, are less so in the study abroad host country (Anderson, 2003). Medina-Lopez-Portillo (2004) found that male study abroad students in Mexico showed gains in intercultural sensitivity in ways that the women in the same program did not.

As presented earlier, some researchers have found that women and men have different experiences when studying abroad, both predeparture and during the program. If that was the case for the participants in this research study, it was not reflected in any significant difference in their MID scores pre- to post-. Intellectual development, at least as studied in this research study, does not seem to be associated with any significant gender differences.

Question 3a: Gains in Intellectual Development for
English and Foreign Language Country Locations

3. Did any of the following variables impact gains made in intellectual development?

a. Language of study abroad country

Examining changes in MID scores (pre- to post-) over one semester for the subgroups studying in English language countries and foreign language countries showed no evidence that mean scores for either post group were higher than the respective pre-group, for both paired sample and 2-sample t tests. Tables 4.7 and 4.8 present those results.

As shown in Tables 4.7 and 4.8, for both the English and foreign language country students, mean pre- and post-MID scores were not significantly different. There is no evidence from this study that students participating in study abroad programs in English language countries or foreign language countries saw significant gains in intellectual development.

The language of the study abroad country has been cited by researchers (Engle & Engle, 2003; Vande Berg et al., 2004) as an important defining characteristic of study abroad programs. Results for the spring 2004 study group of 226 students show that there are

TABLE 4.7
Mean Scores Pre- to Post- for English Language Locations

	Paired			2-Sample		
	M	SD	n	M	SD	n
Pre-	3.08	0.34	42	3.05	0.34	54
Post-	3.08	0.27	42	3.03	0.31	79
p	0.95			0.73		

TABLE 4.8
Mean Scores Pre- to Post- for Foreign Language Locations

	Paired			2-Sample		
	M	SD	n	M	SD	n
Pre-	3.10	0.35	43	3.06	0.39	66
Post-	3.10	0.31	43	3.08	0.35	94
p	0.89			0.78		

no significant gains in intellectual development pre- to post- for students who study abroad in foreign language countries. No statistically significant differences were observed for students studying in English-speaking countries.

Study abroad research, to date, has tended to focus on whether or not studying abroad facilitates language learning (Citron, 1995; Rivers, 1998; Thot, 1998), but generally not on the impact that being in a foreign language environment could have on developmental processes. Language learning has been theorized by some linguists as information processing, a cognitive process that can be enhanced by purposeful activities, pedagogical interactions, and teacher-learner engagement (Smith, 1987) and, further, that language learning is influenced both by the characteristics of the learner, such as age and cognitive ability, and his or her social context, such as integration into group learning strategies (Doughty, 1987). Despite this cognitively challenging foreign language experience, an experience that some

researchers (Douglas & Jones-Rikkers, 2001) have suggested is associated with an increased appreciation for relativism in students attending foreign language programs, there is no evidence from this research
study suggesting that the language of the study abroad country will
impact gains in intellectual development when studying abroad.

Question 3b: Gains in Intellectual Development
for Immersion-Based and Study Center Programs

3. Do any of the following variables impact gains made in intellectual development?

   b. Amount of cultural immersion

   One variable that is important in determining the amount of
cultural immersion for a study abroad student is the program structure, which will be examined here.
   Examining changes in MID scores (pre- to post-) over one
semester for the subgroups studying in immersion-based programs
(those in which the students study with entirely or mostly students
from the host country, such as a direct placement at a foreign university) and study center programs (those in which students study
with entirely or mostly other U.S. students, such as in a program
center designed for U.S. study abroad students) showed no evidence
that mean scores for either post-group were higher than the respective pre-group, for both paired sample and 2–sample tests. Tables
4.9 and 4.10 present these results.
   A defining characteristic important to study abroad
researchers and professionals (Engle & Engle, 2003) is the structure
of the program, particularly on the fundamental question: Where,
and with whom, are U.S. study abroad students studying? Tradi-
tionally this question has been answered in one of two ways: either
in a U.S. study center (or island) program, or in a direct immersion
(direct enrollment) program at a foreign university. While more
sophisticated classifications are emerging (Engle & Engle, 2003),
these two broad descriptors are still commonly used.
   As with the earlier variables, this study does not provide evidence that program structure, particularly participating in a direct

TABLE 4.9
Mean Scores Pre- to Post- for Immersion-Based Programs

	Paired			2-Sample		
	M	SD	n	M	SD	n
Pre-	3.04	0.35	38	3.04	0.40	44
Post-	3.15	0.29	38	3.07	0.30	59
p	0.12			0.64		

TABLE 4.10
Mean Scores Pre- to Post- for Study Center Programs

	Paired			2-Sample		
	M	SD	n	M	SD	n
Pre-	3.13	0.35	47	3.07	0.35	76
Post-	3.04	0.28	47	3.05	0.34	114
p	0.15			0.71		

immersion program over an island program, contributes to gains in intellectual development when studying abroad. One possible reason is that, as Citron (1996) found, direct enrollment in a foreign university program does not necessarily mean that students will be culturally immersed or challenged any more so than their counterparts in U.S. study center programs.

As shown previously in Tables 4.9 and 4.10, mean MID scores for the pre- and post-groups were not significantly different. This was true for both the paired sample and the 2–sample tests over both the immersion-based program students and the study center program students. An additional 2–sample t-test was performed testing the pre scores for both groups of students to verify that there were no differences in the pre-score level. The results showed that at the .05 level, there was no significant difference ($p = 0.74$, $t = -0.33$) in pre-scores for students attending immersion-based programs and those attending study center programs.

*Question 3c: Gains in Intellectual Development
and Previous International Travel*

3. Did any of the following variables impact gains made in intellectual development?

   c. Previous international experience

Students were asked if prior to their study abroad semester they had traveled internationally and, if yes, what the length was of their longest trip abroad. This question was useful in segregating the data from those students for whom studying abroad was their first trip abroad and those for whom it was not. In addition, it separated those who may have traveled abroad briefly from those who had experienced more lengthy international travel. Mean MID scores (pre- to post-) and t-test results for each group are presented in Tables 4.11 and 4.12.

TABLE 4.11
Mean Scores Pre- to Post- for Students with Previous International Travel

	Paired			2-Sample		
	M	*SD*	*n*	*M*	*SD*	*n*
Pre-	3.13	0.32	56	3.12	0.35	80
Post-	3.11	0.30	56	3.10	0.34	108
p	0.71			0.71		

TABLE 4.12
Mean Scores Pre- to Post- for Students with No Previous International Travel

	Paired			2-Sample		
	M	*SD*	*n*	*M*	*SD*	*n*
Pre-	3.00	0.39	29	2.93	0.38	40
Post-	3.05	0.27	29	2.99	0.29	66
p	0.58			0.41		

As shown in Tables 4.11 and 4.12, examining changes in MID scores (pre- to post-) over one semester for the subgroups indicating that they had or had not traveled abroad prior to their study abroad semester showed no evidence that mean scores for either post-group were higher than the respective pre-group, for both paired sample and 2-sample tests.

Since many students who had indicated on the accompanying questionnaire that studying abroad was not their first international travel also indicated that their prior international travel was of a very short duration (1 day, 1 week, 10 days, etc.), I further segregated the data into two subgroups for analysis. One group was comprised of those students who had traveled abroad for 2 weeks or longer. The other group was composed of those who had not traveled abroad combined with those whose international travel was less than 2 weeks. Tests were conducted on mean MID scores (pre- to post-) for both groups, and no significant differences were observed pre- to post- for either group.

However, in observing the pre- and post-score data for the research question pertaining to the previous international travel of study participants, it appeared that those students who had traveled abroad prior to studying abroad had higher pre-scores than those who had not. I conducted a series of 2-sample t-tests to determine whether any differences could be observed in the pre-score and post-score for the groups. The results are presented in Table 4.13.

The results presented in Table 4.13 show that students who had traveled abroad prior to their study abroad semester for any length of time had both significantly higher pre-scores and higher post-scores than those who had not engaged in such travel. However, this result likely does not accurately represent the students' prior experiences abroad because it includes those students traveling abroad for very short durations.

When defining previous international travel in such a way that does not include short trips abroad, such as vacation travel, day trips, and any trip that is not at least 2 weeks' duration, a different result occurred. *Students who had traveled abroad previously for 2 weeks or longer still had significantly higher pre-scores than their less-traveled peers, but their post-scores were not statistically different. In other words, students for whom study abroad was their first meaningful*

TABLE 4.13
Pre- and Post-Scores for Students
with and with No Previous International Travel

	No	Yes	n	p	No + 2	Yes + 2	n	p
Pre-	2.93	3.12	no = 40 yes = 80	0.01*	2.94	3.14	no = 50 yes = 70	0.00*
SD	0.38	0.35			0.37	0.35		
Post-	2.99	3.10	no = 66 yes = 108	0.02*	3.03	3.08	no = 84 yes = 90	0.30
SD	0.29	0.34			0.35	0.30		

Note: No = no international travel before studying abroad; Yes = yes, international travel before studying abroad; No + 2 = no prior international travel or travel of less than 2 weeks; Yes + 2 = prior travel of 2 weeks or more.

*$p < .05$.

international experience caught up to their more experienced peers after one semester abroad.

This finding yields some evidence to support the idea that previous international experience impacts the intellectual development that can occur when studying abroad. A review of the literature on this topic (Farrell & Suvedi, 2003; Martin & Rohrlich, 1991) showed that when analyzing the prior international travel of study abroad students, researchers have distinguished between those students with very short international experiences (such as a day trip to Canada or Mexico, a week's vacation overseas, etc.) and those with longer durations abroad. I chose 2 weeks as an appropriate cutoff because it would likely capture students whose overseas travel was for vacation or recreation only, likely without structured, sustained, and purposeful cultural interactions.

Students with previous international travel experience of 2 weeks or more scored significantly higher on their pre-scores than those students without such previous international travel. However, their post-scores showed no statistical difference. This means that students without meaningful previous international travel experience started off at lower intellectual developmental levels, but that after one semester of studying abroad that gap had become insignificant.

Other researchers, while not focusing on the intellectual development of study abroad students, found insightful answers to related questions that may help us understand the finding presented in this book. Martin and Rohrlich (1991) found that students with no or limited previous international travel began studying abroad with greater concerns over such aspects of studying abroad as adjusting to new customs, food, transportation, and currency. Anderson (2003) found that students with less previous international travel experience initially balked at adjusting to new customs, dress, and behavioral expectations more so than those with previous experience traveling overseas.

Wexler (2006) asserted that a direct encounter with a foreign culture can be associated with cognitive dissonance, mental discomfort over the confusing cultural signposts and other newly encountered and processed information. Wexler's psychological and biological approach holds the possibility of explaining why study abroad students who are first-time international travelers are the ones who gain relative to their peers. This approach will be explored fully in chapter 5.

My research finding, combined with the evidence from the studies cited earlier, suggests that students who have never traveled abroad, or who have done so for very short durations, may be more challenged initially by the overseas experience. This challenge may result in a pattern of intellectual development that shows greater gains than those who have had considerable prior international travel. It was not possible to determine why those with no, or limited, previous international travel had significantly lower pre-scores. The possible reasons for this are complex and were not investigated in this study. Nonetheless, it is possible and compelling to think that the experience of considerable international travel itself leads to a higher level of intellectual development. More research is needed on this topic before that conclusion should be drawn, however, but the results of this study combined with what we know about human interactions in foreign environments make for that interesting argument, as will be addressed in chapter 5.

CHAPTER 5

Challenge of a Lifetime

"'Each day, Sancho,' said Don Quixote, 'you are becoming less doltish and more wise.'"
—Cervantes, *Don Quixote*

What are the benefits of studying abroad? We return now to that
central question, posed in the Introduction to this book. We know
that studying abroad is increasing in popularity on American college and university campuses, now totaling well over 200,000
annual participants. We know too that studying abroad is changing, as students from all majors are incorporating studying abroad
into their academic programs in countries all over the world during all four years of their college life. We know that study abroad
time is shortening, as programs lasting less than one semester are
now the majority nationwide. And we know that studying abroad
is usually, but not always, advocated by study abroad professionals,
the faculty, and senior university leaders as an activity that pro-
motes the understanding of cultures, languages, international
awareness, and global forces.

If there is any criticism of studying abroad it tends to be cen-
tered around the charge that as an academic program it lacks
demonstrable disciplinary learning outcomes and is excused from
the normal rigor expected of other university offerings, what I
referred to earlier as "academic lite." In the first case, the criticism
that studying abroad lacks demonstrable disciplinary learning outcomes, this may very well prove to be a relic of the discipline-
focused undergraduate experience. Interdisciplinary courses, majors,
and undergraduate programs are now so common on campus that
their defense is less and less necessary; indeed, it could be said that
defending the unitary discipline is more necessary today, but that is
not the focus of this book. I argue here that the analysis of studying

abroad as an endeavor tied to one single major or academic discipline is no longer relevant to the discussion of study abroad assessment. Any study abroad advisor worth her or his salt knows to turn a question such as "What study abroad is good for history majors?" into a teachable moment that both helps her or his student explore the vast array of study abroad options available and, perhaps delicately at first, helps the student begin to understand that the choice of major does not drive all other decisions.

The second criticism, that study abroad is "academic lite," is more serious and is a concern that many in the study abroad profession share with some of their faculty colleagues. Perhaps because of the unusual amounts of attention from campus media, or the quantity of glossy flyers and advertisements on our bulletin boards, or perhaps because of the age of globalization in which we live, studying abroad is something that more and more students and parents are expecting as part of the undergraduate experience. That it can be perceived by anyone as little more than a superficial addressing of complex material while jaunting from museums to ruins or, worse, that it is a party-filled journey of excess and expense that produces little from our students except digital photos and "It was awesome!" summary judgments, should make all of us who care about studying abroad pause and address seriously the subject of what our students achieve through study abroad programs.

Earlier in this book I argued that traditional methods of assessing study abroad programs, focused on language learning and gains in country-specific knowledge, are less relevant today, especially because programs are shortening. How much of a foreign language can a student be expected to attain in one winter session or spring break program abroad? How much country-specific knowledge can a student achieve from a tour bus? And if this is the case, or at least the perception, then does this reflect poorly on studying abroad as a rigorous academic endeavor worthy of our collective support? Clearly new approaches to study abroad assessment are overdue.

Yet the vexing questions of *how* study abroad programs can be assessed and *what* specific learning outcomes result from these programs remain with us. In the earlier chapters I discussed how complex studying abroad is as an academic program, with variations in program location, program length, the language of the country chosen for study, program housing and immersion options, and so on. As a research subject, the "treatment" called studying abroad does not lend itself to easy analysis.

Changing Our Own Perspective

What if we looked elsewhere? What if we changed our lenses and asked different questions about studying abroad? Instead of rehashing the question "Are students learning what they should be learning about France (or Mexico, or China, or South Africa)?," what if we asked "How are our students changing for the better?" What if we no longer forced studying abroad into intercultural and linguistic straightjackets, concepts whose definitions seem to be in flux, and sense of importance under duress, from global forces and the digital generation anyway? Instead, what if we freed ourselves to accept that studying abroad is still the best way to learn languages and cultures, that if our students do not return from France (or Mexico, or China, or South Africa) knowing something more about the culture and language of those places than before then something is seriously wrong—and then move on to what else studying abroad can be?

In chapter 1 I cited years of anecdotal perceptions and practitioner observations of how returning study abroad students seem different, changed, to their advisors, professors, and friends. Historians of study abroad programs note that, from its earliest days, study abroad leaders noticed in their returning students a "'broader conception,' 'a new outlook,' and 'an objective viewpoint'" (Hoffa, 2007, p. 81). These descriptions need not be based on cultural appreciation, or a sense of history, or any other disciplinary approach, nor do they require a link to gains in foreign language ability. Something else is, and has been, going on with study abroad students, and this book is an attempt to help us understand what that might be.

What if by having a "broader conception" the study abroad student is actually showing evidence of intellectual development? What if that "objective viewpoint" is a sign that she or he understands that knowledge and expertise can come from multiple sources now, whether lecturing to her or him on campus or interacting with her or him on the streets of Sydney? What if his or her "new outlook" is not only worldliness in style or humor but perhaps is a recognition on his or her part that knowledge is a relative concept influenced by context and experience, whether from his or her hometown in upstate New York or his or her host family's hometown in northern Spain? What if by "different, changed" we are actually noting that our returning study abroad students cannot go back to their earlier, less intellectually advanced ways of knowing, and that this irreversible development, as William Perry called it, distinguishes them from both their peers and their earlier selves?

In chapter 4 I showed that, on most variables important to the study abroad profession, namely, program structure, language, and degree of cultural immersion, there were no statistically significant differences in intellectual development from pre- to post-program in students when looking at these variations in participation. I also showed that there was no difference based on gender. The only significant difference observed in this study was the variable of previous international travel. In chapter 4 I showed that students for whom studying abroad was their first meaningful international experience actually began study abroad programs at a statistically lower level of intellectual development than their more internationally mobile peers. Likewise, students with prior travel abroad for a substantial amount of time (at least 2 weeks) began study abroad programs at a statistically higher level of intellectual development than their less-experienced peers. The significant finding from this study was that by the end of their study abroad semester, those less internationally experienced students had erased that statistical gap. I call this "the first time effect."

The First Time Effect

Why might this be occurring? Why would this first meaningful international exposure be associated with growth in intellectual development? And might it help us understand why studying abroad is such an eye-opening experience for our students? We know from the work of William Perry that during the college years students must actively make meaning out of their increasingly complex experiences. This meaning making process, this construction of an internal dialogue and worldview, occurs in interaction with the environment and must increasingly incorporate encounters with diversity. These encounters are typically a good thing, ones that often are deliberately designed into freshman seminars, residence life experiences, senior capstones, and the like. Indeed, most colleges state that the understanding of diversity in some form is a goal of the undergraduate experience, as is an enhanced ability to think critically. But these experiences also can produce stress and anxiety, as previously held beliefs and approaches to knowledge and expertise have to be questioned by the student. Perry found that some undergraduates found this a joyful and liberating process, while others did not.

I argue here that studying abroad is an activity that challenges students by forcing an intense encounter with diversity. I also argue that studying abroad is replete with stress, anxiety, and intellectual discomfort by deliberately exposing students to alternative environments that require an alternate worldview, and that this is done in a substantive, meaningful way. Lastly, I argue that, as evidenced in this study, this intellectual tension is particularly acute during the first sojourn abroad and may lead to significant gains in intellectual development in participating students, what I call "the first time effect." This approach to assessing the benefits of studying abroad has not been promoted in this way before.

It may not be surprising that college students who also are first-time international travelers are impacted in this way if we look for a moment for guidance outside the fields of studying abroad and higher education. In his book *Brain and Culture*, Bruce Wexler, noted Yale University psychiatrist, identifies the role of social interaction in creating internal psychological structures. Drawing from studies in biology as well as psychology, Wexler concludes that society and culture have a great influence on how a person's brain and mind will work. Of particular importance to the development of cognitive function, says Wexler, is the input of sensory stimulation. This stimulation can be as basic as a mother's touch and as complex as exposure to a second language. These inputs are believed to be necessary for the development of the human brain, and the processing of these sensory inputs shapes the particulars of brain structure and function (Wexler, 2006).

As relates to intellectual development that may occur when studying abroad, Wexler states that one crucial aspect of human cognitive development is the resistance to change that begins to take place in young adulthood. He refers to this as a time when perceptual, attitudinal, and cognitive structures resist change and people try to surround themselves with the familiar, eschewing foreign elements into their environments. Wexler cites two examples of potentially difficult and traumatic experiences that are typically beyond an individual's ability to maintain the normal fit, the normal ability to make meaning out of experience based on the individual's current worldview: mourning the loss of a loved one, and the meeting of different cultures (Wexler, 2006).

The experience of crossing cultures is fraught with scary and seemingly nonsensical daily encounters. A common reaction is for individuals to deny their insertion into the new culture, instead preferring to build a life similar to their previous one. Even though study abroad students have voluntarily chosen this experience, we have all seen students who retreat to the comfort of their American friends (now made all the more possible with enhanced electronic and telephonic communications), favorite television shows, or a visit to the fast food restaurant. Seen this way, these students are behaving normally by cushioning the shock of the new as they gradually push their way into a different, foreign culture.

The "uncomfortable dissonance" described by Wexler (2006, p. 10) is subjective. The newcomer, in this case the American student, is, after all, in the same place receiving the same information as her or his new countrymen and women, and those people feel no such discomfort. Those people native to the study abroad country are making meaning out of their daily experiences in ways that are culturally defined as meaningful, even if at first nonsensical to the recently arrived student. In this sense, the discomfort and dissonance that many call "culture shock" are not feelings simply to be overcome but rather are part of a process of cognitive growth whereby people, including our study abroad students, can start to make sense of the new information and knowledge coming at them.

They do this by immersing themselves in the culture where this information and knowledge reside, by confronting their initial confusion over it, and by beginning to surmount their rigid defenses against it.

Our Students in Context

Some examples from my research might assist in our understanding of these processes. Consider the example of an American study abroad student attending a program in Hong Kong, China. One difference he observed immediately was that there was no legal drinking age of 21. How did he and his friends react?:

> [Y]ou don't need an ID to drink, there's no 21. We were really psyched at the beginning, and everyone got really drunk the first nights and then we were like, what are we doing? We're here in China, we can drink anytime we want when we get back to the States. We traveled half way around the world *to drink*? To get drunk? And not be able to experience, to see the Forbidden City in China? or to walk down the street. This is probably the first and only time I will actually walk down this street, and shake these people's hands.

The student's statement that here "there's no 21," is obviously wrong. People in China turn 21 years old every day. What he clearly meant was that there was no societal or cultural connection between 21 years old and drinking alcohol legally in his study abroad country. At first, the worldview he brought with him while studying abroad led him down one path: taking advantage of no drinking age by drinking in excess. But then his view changed. If it did not mean anything to be of legal drinking age in China, then why was he attaching any meaning to it? In other words, it seems that his understanding of what a legal drinking age is underwent an important change. That change was caused by his cultural encounter with a foreign society, but the change was internal to him and impacted how he understood what knowledge is and how it is culturally contextual. Further, it appears that this change in understanding led to positive changes in behavior.

An American student reflecting on his semester in London said this:

> [I'm] much more calm. It's cooled me down a little, especially with senior year coming up. I'm more laid back that things will fall into place. It's definitely, the thing I learned is that America is not it, there's so much more out there . . . I think it's just opened me up. . . . Just because we do things in a certain way doesn't mean that it is correct, or right, and it doesn't necessarily mean that there is a wrong or a right, that it's just our culture. You can't go there expecting it to be America because it's just not.

This student experienced studying abroad in an English-speaking city on a large, island program with mostly other American students, and yet it clearly impacted his worldview. His views reflect an enhanced appreciation for the effect of culture on what is perceived as right and wrong, and how instead of being stressful to him, it has calmed him. It is as if his newfound awareness that other societies and cultures are organized in profoundly different ways now makes his own society and culture more understandable. There are probably other examples from his life in the United States that would make more sense to him now too. He is not necessarily comparing his American experiences to life in England, but he seems more aware that knowledge and information are constantly coming at him, that it is all subject to processing and interpretation, that it is very often culturally defined and contextually based, and that now he is more equipped to manage it.

Wexler wrote that "[t]he relationship between the individual and the environment is so extensive that it almost overstates the distinction between the two to speak of a relationship at all" (Wexler, 2006, p. 39). If a person's worldview and information processing structures are so linked to his or her social environment, then it is no wonder that placing that person in a new and different environment is uncomfortable. Because of this discomfort, after a certain point most people seek to avoid it. That point is typically in early adulthood, says Wexler, after the onset of sexual maturity and when the adult brain possesses a reduced ability to change:

[A]fter reaching puberty, imitative shaping of the brain to features of the environment is decreased, and as a result the individual becomes more set in his ways; a sense of individual identity begins to crystallize, and the relationship between the individual and his environment begins to change. Increasingly, energy and effort are spent acting on the environment, or positioning oneself within the environment so as to maintain the symmetry and parallels between inner structure and outer reality. (Wexler, 2006, pp. 118–119)

Wexler cites the example of language learning and how it is vastly easier for children to learn a second language than for adults. Among the activities or occurrences Wexler cites that can force the individual to confront challenging and uncomfortable change is entering into a new, foreign society. In this new environment a problem may not be able to be recognized, let alone solved in the appropriate way, causing strain and internal discomfort. My argument is that studying abroad, for students never before exposed to this intensely different cultural environment, can serve as such a challenging and discomforting experience that it forces the student to modify existing mental processes toward new meaning-making structures. For some students, this leads to a measurable increase in intellectual development.

It is important to point out here that I am not arguing that the learning of cultural differences, or foreign languages, or country-specific knowledge per se is the cause of this development in first-time sojourners. I am arguing that it is the intense international experience itself that leads to this individual growth, growth driven by what Wexler describes as "the extended and arduous effort required to restructure the internal world so that it matches the new external world" (Wexler, 2006, p. 144). The act of restructuring internal meaning-making structures in the face of pronounced changes in the external environment could be the process that some students go through during their first international sojourn, a process that can lead, as evidenced in this book, to demonstrable gains in intellectual development for those individuals.

Seen this way, might college student intellectual development be an example of, as L. S. Vygotsky wrote, the "buds or flowers of development rather than the fruits of development" (Vygotsky, 1978, p. 86) that can mature only when the individual is in the proper learning environment? Vygotsky, the prominent Russian psychologist, believed that development to higher levels of mental function occurs in concert with learning, not that learning always follows development in sequential fashion, and that this development takes place in interaction with other people in the culture around us. With an appropriate learning structure and environment, developmental processes are set in motion that would be impossible to produce otherwise (Vygotsky, 1978). We know from our practice that study abroad students typically are active participants within their new cultural milieu, not typically as tourists but as students, volunteers, interns, and members of the family. As William Perry observed with his study of undergraduate students, this active engagement is joyful to some and extremely challenging to others. The argument presented in this book is that those students who have not previously had to engage in such an intensely new cultural encounter, and for whom studying abroad represents their first meaningful international experience, are the ones who gain in their intellectual abilities relative to their peers. When placed in the context of prior research, this result should not surprise us and in fact might have been predictable. It also shows how powerful studying abroad can be as an academic endeavor, even beyond the intercultural and linguistic gains that it produces and for what it is more typically known.

Impact beyond Study Abroad

Back on campus, it is possible that this development can have spillover benefits into other aspects of our students' academic lives. If a student's intellectual development receives a kick-start through the intensely challenging international experience, then she or he might think and question in a more critical way. Researchers (Ennis, 1993; Petress, 2004) in the field of critical thinking cite students' ability to evaluate information better, often through observation and experience, as an indicator of improved critical thinking, an effect on students noted by study abroad leaders decades ago (Hoffa, 2007). The process of listening to reasoned arguments, judging the credibility of sources, and being careful not to draw simplistic or hasty conclusions shows evidence of enhanced critical thinking. While not the same as intellectual development, some outcomes of intellectual development, such as understanding that there are multiple sources of expertise, compare to enhanced critical thinking ability that values healthy skepticism and a tentative approach in accepting others' claims. It is reasonable to suggest that as a student develops intellectually, she or he also builds the potential to think critically, because she or he now possesses an internal cognitive structure less resistant to change and more aware of the need to hear others' views, even if they challenge a previously held belief.

It also is noteworthy that critical thinking researchers (Douglas, 2000) indicate that the human tendency to resist new information and to hold onto existing beliefs (belief perseverance) must be recognized and overcome in order for students to improve their ability to think critically. In much the same way that Wexler described how difficult it is for people to change the way they think and process information once in early adulthood, it seems that our stubborn, entrenched intellectual patterns are only overcome with considerable effort. Entering into a new culture, and having to make meaning out of foreign cues, is one method of challenging our existing belief systems and internal meaning-making structures and therefore has the potential to enhance our students' critical thinking ability too. Study abroad pioneers as far back as the 1920s believed that this was happening (Hoffa, 2007), and higher education would benefit from a more thorough investigation of this possible link.

Review and Discussion

The purpose of the research study presented in this book was to explore the possibility that studying abroad was associated with gains in intellectual development for participating students. While there is some evidence that this occurs for some students, particularly those with little or no prior international exposure, there also is considerable evidence that most students did not realize these gains. What can we say about this? And are there ways that studying abroad might be designed to foster the intellectual development of study abroad students in an intentional way?

Engle and Engle (2003) posited that study abroad researchers have begun to reorient their work away from analyzing the sheer numbers of participants and toward the quality and nature of the study abroad experience. Vande Berg, Balkcum, Scheid, and Whalen (2004) asked, as study abroad enrollment numbers continue to rise each year, "What is it that our students are learning while abroad?" (Vande Berg et al., 2004, p. 102). That researchers and practitioners in the study abroad field continue to ask these basic questions, and strive to organize and classify studying abroad in ways that are systematically observable, shows that there is little consensus still on how to best define studying abroad and how to best study its effects. Even as a greater emphasis within the study abroad profession is being placed on program classifications and outcomes, there also is the concurrent recognition that it can be daunting to generalize about goals and outcomes for all students in a way that is too generic, that "desired and real outcomes are as individual as the students themselves, each with her or his unique life tale, motivation, and imagined future" (Engle & Engle, 2003, p. 5).

My research study attempted to contribute to the ongoing discussion of study abroad program outcomes and how distinctions in program type can impact how students change when studying abroad. However, as was shown in chapter 4, I can say little definitively about how *all* students changed after one semester's study abroad participation. What I can say is that some students showed gains in intellectual development level, and some students did not. Also, I can say that some students began studying abroad at a significantly lower intellectual development level than others, and that students who had traveled abroad prior to studying abroad began at a higher level of intellectual development than their peers. Lastly, I can say that this difference disappeared after one semester, so that students who began at a significantly lower level of intellectual development ended studying abroad at the same level as their peers.

As Engle and Engle (2003) stated earlier, there is reason to believe that outcomes from studying abroad are as individual as the students themselves. In much the same way, it seems that the results of my research study are not able to show that studying abroad affects all students the same way regarding their intellectual development.

The variables chosen in my study, including the language of the study abroad country, the amount of cultural immersion built into the program, and housing choice, have all been cited in current literature as important variables upon which to define program type and to measure the impact of the study abroad experience (Engle & Engle, 2003; Vande Berg et al., 2004). Further, prior research on studying abroad (Carlson et al., 1990; Sharma & Mulka, 1993; Sutton & Rubin, 2004) has shown that some study abroad students show gains in abilities and awareness that provide useful comparisons to the intellectual development defined by Perry's (1968) model. These factors combined to provide a useful context for this research study. However, it is worth repeating that this study did not produce findings that show evidence that *all* students showed gains in intellectual development when studying abroad. Below are some possible explanations why this might have occurred.

Short Time Period of Study

One possible explanation for the lack of significant gains in intellectual development for all participating students when studying abroad is the relatively short duration of the time period under study. Intellectual development is a complex process for which one semester may not be sufficient time to observe changes, or to assign causality to any observed changes.

Baxter Magolda (1992) used a longitudinal research design that included her undergraduates' entire college experience, from the first semester to beyond graduation, to ensure that the totality of the undergraduate experience, including the study abroad experience, was reflected in any conclusions. Some study abroad researchers (Vande Berg et al., 2004) have advocated a third (pre-post-post/post) survey administration months after students' return to campus to allow for reflection on the study abroad experience. These researchers wonder if some time is required for the impact of studying abroad to be measured. The research study presented here was a panel study over one semester. It is possible that only one semester studying abroad did not provide the time for participant reflection necessary for gains in intellectual development to become apparent in all students, or to account for the entirety of the experience of how studying abroad contributes to a student's undergraduate career.

During a semester of 12 to 15 weeks, it is not uncommon for students in any setting to realize no gains in intellectual development. Gains that do occur are usually associated with intentional programming or course components, such as reflective journals, group discussions, and capstone, integrative activities. There is no evidence that, overall, studying abroad itself served as one of those deliberate activities that fosters intellectual development for all students. Without these intentional program components, the short duration of the one-semester study abroad program may be insufficient for most students to realize gains in their intellectual development; instead, a longer time period of study might be necessary for them to see significant gains. However, first-time sojourners did realize a gain relative to their peers, suggesting that for these students the intensely challenging international exposure is a sufficient prompt for growth in intellectual development. Discussed later in this chapter is how studying abroad might be organized and designed to incorporate more deliberate activities that foster intellectual development for more students, even those with considerable prior international experience.

Recall that the students who had traveled abroad prior to studying abroad had significantly higher MID pre-scores over those who had not, but their post-scores were statistically the same. This suggests that the students who did not travel internationally had caught up to those who had after one semester of study abroad. It is possible, then, that there are some benefits to intellectual development that simply come from prolonged exposure to an international environment. Whereas there is no evidence in this study to suggest that any one study abroad program type is more beneficial to intellectual development than another, there is at least some evidence that international exposure prior to studying abroad is associated with higher MID scores.

One intriguing and unanswered question resulting from this study is this: Why did the students who had previous international travel experience, and whose MID scores were significantly higher, not continue to maintain a significantly higher level of intellectual development after one semester studying abroad? In other words, why were the lower-level students able to catch up with those who began at a higher level? One possibility is that those students who had previous international travel experience were not as intellectually challenged as those for whom studying abroad was their first meaningful contact with a foreign culture. These more experienced students' discomfort and dissonance, as described by Wexler, might have been less than that of the first-time sojourners. It may be necessary, therefore, to build in other programmatic components to studying abroad that will challenge this group of students. More on this topic will be presented later in this chapter.

Instrument Chosen

The MID is an example of a *production task*, defined as a task in which the individual is asked to produce spontaneously a response based on his or her current skills, abilities, and cognitive competencies (King, 1990). This differs from a *recognition task*, in that this latter task, in the case of intellectual development, asks students to choose on a Likert scale items that they consider significant to their own ideal learning environment (Moore, 1989). In this case, the MID asks the student to write a fairly long essay about his or her classroom preferences, teaching style preferences, and, in the post instrument, to reflect on what he or she thought was learned during the preceding semester.

The advantage of using a production task is that it typically yields rich and complex information about the respondent's capacities. Its primary disadvantage, however, is that in asking for such thoughtful responses from students, it is sometimes difficult for students to respond when they have not thought about the topic before, or cannot express their complex views in words (King, 1990). Since this was a voluntary study conducted via the Internet, this complex instrument also may have discouraged some students from participating.

For the reasons just cited, the production task MID, while overall a very useful and proven tool, might not capture for all students the development toward the next Perry position and might have missed what positive changes did occur in students' intellectual development. Researchers (Fischer & Silvern, 1985) believe that competence at one stage does not always mean that the individual has the ability to perform at that stage; the individual must be "activated or primed" (Fischer & Silvern, 1985, p. 621) in order to achieve performance reflective of this new developmental level. King (1990) described "readiness for change" (King, 1990, p. 83) in the individual, and conducive environmental factors around the individual, as being necessary for advancement to the next stage of intellectual development. It is possible that not all students participating in this research study were able to represent their true capacities through the instrument chosen, or were not sufficiently primed by the experience leading up to taking the post-instrument, so any development gains were not observed.

Intensity of Treatment

Related to the possible lack of a student's readiness for change is the question of the intensity of the treatment undertaken. Intellectual development occurs in interaction with the environment (King 1990; Perry, 1968), therefore, it is possible that if the environmental factors of the treatment are not of sufficient intensity, then the student will not develop to the next stage.

The fact that the overwhelming majority of students in the study, over 88%, studied abroad in the countries of Western Europe and Australia/New Zealand, countries with advanced economies and Western cultures, may impact the question of intensity. Since development requires a challenge, and intellectual development in particular occurs in interaction with the environment, it is possible that one of the reasons for the lack of significant intellectual development in the majority of participating students is that their study abroad experiences were not as challenging due to their participation in largely Western countries and cultures that were more similar to their own. Perhaps, if they had studied and lived in countries more different than their own they might have experienced changes in MID scores.

Researchers (Mines, et al., 1990) have cited that failure to develop to the next stage of intellectual development can be related to a lack of environmental opportunities to practice and use such skills. Further, it is best when cognitive skills are modeled and taught to students, with the opportunity for feedback in the application of these new abilities (King, 1990). It is possible, then, that the study abroad experience was not structured so that opportunities were present for students specifically to practice and refine their cognitive abilities, thus leading to a lack of evidence for this development overall regarding this study.

Researchers on intellectual development in college students note that the biggest typical gains in MID scores come in the first year and just before graduation, often in conjunction with deliberate treatments such as first-year seminars or senior capstone courses (W. S. Moore, personal communication, April 27, 2005). In this research study, 89% (76 out of 85) of the students completing both the pre- and the post-instruments were juniors or seniors. Of those, the most common year represented was the junior year, and there was no evidence that the study abroad programs were structured in such a way to deliberately promote intellectual development.

Study Abroad Designed to Promote Intellectual Development

As stated earlier, there was no evidence that the students participating in this research study took part in study abroad programs that were designed, or even possessed components that were designed, to foster intellectual development in intentional ways. As study abroad programs continue to grow, and with it the concomitant interest in assessing outcomes, how can these programs be designed to promote intellectual development?

A possible answer to this question can come from what is currently known about intellectual development and how educational experiences can be structured to maximize the potential for such development to occur. As has been cited, intellectual development is the process of making meaning out of experience and confrontations with diversity (Perry, 1968), and it occurs in interaction with the environment (King, 1990). Dewey (1916) pioneered the notion that education results from experience and championed the process of noting results from experience that were not noted previously as a method for increasing ability for subsequent experiences. Kolb (1984) described a cycle of experiential learning involving active participation, reflection, integration, and problem solving. And researchers in service learning (Jacoby & Associates, 1996) cite the essential component of student reflection on experience, including class discussions and journal writing, when designing programs explicitly designed to foster learning and development.

Citron's (1996) work in study abroad programs showed that faculty involvement when studying abroad can lead to better integration of the study abroad experience into the participating students' knowledge of the host country. He found that students taking part in a program without a well-structured orientation and without faculty guidance during the program were left to process the experience by themselves, often resulting in superficial approaches to understanding.

It is possible that by structuring study abroad programs to foster intentionally the intellectual development of participating students, the gains that appeared for some of my student participants might be realized for many more. One change could be to incorporate deliberate and more structured faculty-student involvement. For example, by requiring student journals, ones that allow for the reflection and processing of the study abroad experience, and group discussions, including those occurring online with faculty advisors at home, study abroad administrators and faculty could begin to see and gauge student intellectual development on studying abroad in more precise and deliberate ways. By adding discussion questions to required readings and structured discussion time to study abroad orientation weeks and study tours, students would be encouraged to process their new observations and experiences toward making new meaning out of them. This process would be aided by the experienced faculty directors of the program, who would preselect discussion items and reflection topics based on their knowledge of the country, thus providing the necessary structure and support for intellectual development to occur.

Widick and Knefelkamp identified four variables underlying the intellectual developmental model as applied to college students:

(1) the student's experience with and response to diversity; (2) the amount of structure in the learning environment; (3) the nature of experiential learning that was a part of the learning experience; and (4) the degree to which the experience was able to be related to the context of the students' lives (Knefelkamp, 2003). Further, Knefelkamp (2003) cited the need for recognition and understanding of the students by program administrators and faculty during an experience in order to show the respect and encouragement that make it possible for the student involved to endure the stress of intellectual growth.

In this regard, and as applied to intellectual development, the ideas presented earlier for structuring study abroad programs to impact intellectual development in a more deliberate way are not unlike those undertaken in other parts of the university. Whether on campus or not, learning experiences can and are being reexamined in order to promote desired outcomes such as intellectual development. In this case, study abroad programs could be reexamined and restructured to promote the intellectual development of participating students in ways that are more intentional. In so doing, gains may be seen in more participating students that are able to be measured, as was seen in this study for some.

Implications for Studying Abroad and Higher Education

The Complex Nature of Studying Abroad
and Intellectual Development

One implication of this research study is to confirm that both studying abroad and college student intellectual development are complex and multifaceted. Both defy simple description and require an in-depth approach to understand them. Attempts to classify and categorize studying abroad are gaining momentum (Engle & Engle, 2003), and new ways of studying the long-term impact of studying abroad also are being examined (Vande Berg et al., 2004). These attempts are recent, and while encouraging they are not sufficiently adopted across the study abroad profession so that all practitioners and researchers have incorporated them into their work and research.

For this reason, research questions regarding the impact of study abroad student outcomes on program structure, duration, quality, intensity, and so on, some of which were explored in this study, have little comparable data upon which to base and compare. This research study does not offer encouraging support for the effort to classify study abroad programs by type, insofar as such typology would help us understand how participation in different study abroad program types contributes to intellectual development.

Similarly, college student intellectual development is a complex, multifaceted outcome influenced both by the individual and her or his interactions with the environment. Studying it, and examining possible reasons for it, must be done in a way that appreciates its complexity and does not overstate the impact of any one college activity or program. That said, the finding that students with prior international travel began studying abroad at a higher level of intellectual development suggests areas of further inquiry, some of which will be discussed later.

The Problem of Self-Selection and Generalizability

This research study also suggests that there is considerable self-selection occurring during every step of studying abroad. Beach (1995) commented on the considerable self-selection of students studying abroad, even at high study abroad participation schools. Schroth and McCormack (2000) showed that many study abroad students tend to exhibit characteristics not found in nonstudy abroad students in the areas of motivation and achievement. As long as studying abroad is a voluntary activity, it is likely that it will continue to attract students who are, or consider themselves to be, more internationally oriented, multicultural, tolerant, adventurous, and high achieving (Beach, 1995; Schroth & McCormack, 2000).

Chapter 4 showed that by comparing all pre-scores with the 85 students taking both the pre- and post-test, pre-scores were statistically the same across the sample. This suggests that the pre-post sample was representative of the larger student group involved. Also, it should be noted that those self-selecting to take both the pre- and the post-test differed from those taking the post-test only on the question of program structure—a variable that later proved inconsequential to the research question being studied. Nonetheless, it was not possible to know the MID scores for those students not participating, and it should be noted again that a low number (only 12%) of the possible number of students chose to participate.

It is always difficult to make general observations applicable to all students by only studying a limited group of self-selected students, as was done on this study, however, insofar as the subgroups of the study sample related to the study sample, and how the sample compared with the overall study abroad population, including national comparison groups, I consider the results from this study fairly well reflective of the American study abroad population. That said, caution should be used when applying the results of this study to general college student populations, especially those students not studying abroad. That caution should not prevent us, however, from using these results as another encouragement for increasing study abroad programs on our campuses. What should coincide with this increase is further focus and research on its resulting impact for the greater, and newer, students involved.

Students without Prior International Travel

Lastly, an implication based on this research comes from the analysis regarding students who had not traveled abroad prior to studying abroad. As presented in chapter 4, the group of students who had not traveled internationally (or who had done so for a very short time) prior to studying abroad began their semesters at a significantly lower MID score level than those who had traveled abroad previously for a more considerable duration. This difference disappeared after one semester of studying abroad. That was the one significant finding from the research questions posed in this study.

The implication stemming from this finding is that studying abroad may have its greatest impact on intellectual development, and possibly on other outcome measures as well, for students without lengthy prior international travel experience. These students, when compared to their peers, are at a relatively lower level of intellectual development. Some commentators on studying abroad (Kauffmann et al., 1992) believe that gains on studying abroad do follow this pattern. An implication is that students at lower levels of intellectual development, such as first-year students or students without prior international experience, might benefit most from studying abroad.

It should be noted, however, that there is much we do not know about this group of students. A student's lack of international travel prior to studying abroad could be the result of many socio-economic, cultural, geographic, and familial factors, therefore we should still be cautious about attributing the benefits of studying abroad to that result.

Suggestions for Further Research

Suggestions for further research as a result of this study are those that would seek to enhance our understanding of how studying abroad can contribute to student intellectual development in ways that were not discovered during this study. Of particular interest is the impact that an activity that is complex, diverse, and potentially eye-opening, such as studying abroad, has on students who begin studying abroad at lower levels of intellectual development compared to other students. As found in this study, the only significant difference observed was not pre- to post-test on the study, but for pre-scores of students based on their prior international travel experience.

The relationship between a complex treatment such as study abroad programs and students at lower developmental levels should be explored further. It is possible that studying abroad can benefit all students, but that its impact on intellectual development is mostly realized by students who begin studying abroad at a lower level.

A second, and related, question for further study is this: Why would students who have traveled abroad begin studying abroad already at significantly higher MID score levels? As was introduced earlier in this chapter, there could be numerous possible explanations for this, including socioeconomic factors, the impact of internationally mobile parents, and the possible impact that international travel itself has on cognitive ability. Researchers have referred to disruptions in meaning making that can occur during even relatively short international travels (McNamee & Faulkner, 2001), and how culture shock can lead to a more sophisticated understanding of culture and meaning (Bochner, 1982; Oberg, 1960). If international travel itself has the ability to influence intellectual ability, then this might explain the initial difference in MID scores.

Additional research also is needed about why some students in this study realized gains in MID scores and others did not. The study variables chosen are of common interest to the study abroad profession, particularly program structure and the language of the study abroad country, but there was little, if any, evidence to support the idea that these differences in program offerings shed light on why gains do or do not occur. Intellectual development occurs within the individual in interaction with the environment. It is possible that a different conceptual framework for a study, perhaps one that focused more on the characteristics of students' prior international experiences and their motivations for studying abroad, would lead to a better understanding of this complex question.

Lastly, as study abroad participation rates continue to show that short-term programs (typically defined as programs less than 8 weeks) are gaining in popularity with students and colleges, more research is needed on the impact that such short-term programs have on desired student outcomes. Short-term programs vary considerably in length and structure, including summer programs, winter session programs, and embedded program models involving on-campus portions and faculty-led study abroad portions. With programs as short as 1 week, more research is needed on what impact, if any, can occur over such short durations, regardless of the outcome measure.

A SUNY colleague, experienced in short-term programming at the community college level, commented for this book that she can observe changes in students in programs as short as 10 days. Often, she continued, observable shifts in attitude and approach are seen in as little as just 3 or 4 days abroad. The students to whom she refers take part in well-structured, faculty-led programs that deliberately engage students in direct international study and encounter. While perhaps not universally the case, the findings presented in this book provide encouragement for the practical observations we have made for years regarding the impact that studying abroad has on our students, regardless of program length.

This study produced evidence that prior international travel can be associated with higher intellectual development. Presumably, this result would be seen after students studied abroad for shorter durations as well, making studying abroad itself worthy of continued encouragement as a way to enhance the intellectual development of first-time sojourners on our campuses.

Harnessing Student Motivation

When asked, study abroad professionals often give anecdotal motivations for their students' decisions to study abroad, such as to gain a broader perspective or to learn something that they cannot learn at home. Similarly, as has been discussed in this book, study abroad professionals describe their returning students often in anecdotal ways, such as that they are changed people, more mature and worldly. These attempts at understanding students' motivations and outcomes, while often not rigorously researched, are based on a reserve of knowledge built from our collective action.

Although this research study did not answer directly why study abroad students participate in this type of college experience, study abroad practitioners know from their practice that, for example, a student who took a high school trip to France might be motivated to return to France during college to continue her academic and cultural exploration. Similarly, study abroad practitioners know from their practice that students whose parents or families engage in regular international travel, whether to see family or take part in extended personal journeys, can come to the experience motivated to pursue it with some knowledgeable expectation about its benefits. It is possible that those students who do not possess either the actual or the personally connected international experience are the ones who begin studying abroad at a developmentally lower level. These could be the students who see the biggest gains in intellectual development when studying abroad, possibly because it is their first international experience and therefore has a disproportionate impact on them compared to their more internationally experienced peers.

As I have noted in this book, limited research has been done on student motivation for studying abroad. Engle and Engle (2003) stated that study abroad students tend to be part of two broad groups: those who seek "knowledge-transfer" (Engle & Engle, 2003, p. 4), such as a biology field course abroad, and those who seek to learn more "subjective culture" (Engle and Engle, 2003, p. 4) while abroad, such as the language, values, and patterns of thinking and behaving of the host country. Other than this broad definition, not much more is known about these differing student motivations for studying abroad. No study has been conducted on student intellectual developmental differences for these two groups of study abroad students.

Schroth and McCormack (2000) researched psychological personality dimensions in an attempt to understand more about how study abroad students differ from those not going abroad. They found that study abroad students measured higher on a scale that measured desire for unusual sensations or experiences associated with a nonconformist lifestyle (Schroth & McCormack, 2000). In my professional role as a study abroad practitioner, I regularly collect program evaluations from returning study abroad students in my programs. Among the questions I regularly ask returning students is why they were interested in studying abroad in the first place. A compilation of these questions (McKeown, 2003) showed that students cited a desire to travel and have fun as their top two reasons for studying abroad. Clearly, good research on study abroad student motivation is insufficient, and other researchers (Vande Berg et al., 2004) have made similar calls for further research on student motivation for studying abroad and how it might help us understand more about outcomes.

But if the majority of study abroad students choose to participate because they are sensation seekers looking for travel and fun, and if we know that at least some of those students will increase in intellectual development, then we have much to gain by harnessing this student desire for travel and fun by designing as many study abroad programs as possible. First-time sojourners might initially be only able to take advantage of a short-term program, for example, because of the enormity of the undertaking, the cost, support (or lack thereof) of studying abroad from family and friends, and other important reasons. While most study abroad professionals, myself included, will continue to advocate for as long a study abroad experience as possible,

I believe this study provides the backing that some study abroad is better than none. Instead of worrying that short programs are of little academic value, we can embrace them as a viable vehicle for some students to have that eye-opening experience that we now know can contribute to their intellectual development, as well as all of the other well-documented benefits of studying abroad.

It must be remembered that this research does not address the linguistic and cultural gains of studying abroad. My reasons for not focusing on these areas were established in chapter 1, namely, that these approaches are already fairly well researched and, more importantly, I believe that these approaches are less relevant to today's college experience. Indeed *the first time effect* that I describe in this book focuses on intellectual development in our students instead of on traditional linguistic and cultural measures, because by focusing there we free ourselves to embrace nontraditional study abroad, short-term study abroad, and innovative topics and faculty-led approaches that may or may not incorporate a deliberate component of language, cultural learning, or country-specific knowledge. For these reasons, exploring new ways of assessing study abroad programs, such as measuring intellectual development, is relevant.

Similarly, the widely respected National Survey of Student Engagement (NSSE, 2007) calls for increasing the number of study abroad opportunities for students, regardless of the duration, precisely because of the impact that study abroad programs can have on broad learning outcomes in higher education:

> The length of time spent overseas did not make a difference in the frequency with which students used deep learning approaches after returning to their campus or their self-reported gains.
>
> It appears that the amount of time one is abroad is not as important as whether a student has such an experience. This suggests that there is value in increasing the number of short-term cross-cultural or "study away" opportunities for students who for some reason cannot be away from their home institution for an extended period of time. (NSSE, 2007, p. 17)

I believe study abroad professionals and higher education leaders can use the results of this book to embrace studying abroad in all of its forms, including short-term programming, to enhance the intellectual development of participating students in a way that is especially important to first time sojourners. Seen this way, there is no bad study abroad program per se. There may be bad teaching or poor-quality delivery, but that is no different from higher education on campus. As evidenced by this study, studying abroad is an activity that warrants full-throated encouragement for as many of our students as possible. It involves meaningful, credit-bearing experiences that allow students to gain from the subject matter and destination country, with the added benefit of producing demonstrable gains in intellectual development for first-time sojourners. College and university leaders, as well as study abroad professionals, can use the findings from this study to present studying abroad not only as an opportunity to gain international knowledge and possibly language skills but also as a credit-bearing way to foster intellectual development that can carry over into the students' other courses and academic programs overall.

Conclusion

"'Each day, Sancho,' said Don Quixote, 'you are becoming less doltish and more wise'" (Cervantes, 1957). The findings of this research study give us some encouragement that studying abroad leads to significant gains in intellectual development for students with little or no meaningful international exposure. In fact, no significant findings pre- to post-program were observed for any other research question posed.

Statistics and research methods aside, whether in a study abroad office on any campus or in a theater during Cervantes' time, most people would agree that something positive and lasting occurs in the mind as a result of a meaningful international experience.

People have been crossing borders into foreign places for all time, and there can only be one first time for each person. In Cervantes' classic, Sancho Panza was curious and willing to travel, but he was considered simple next to his more worldly companion, and at times afraid of the adventure unfolding in front of him. His progression as a character belied those simple attributes, and his background did not prevent him from becoming a more sophisticated person as a result of his exotic travels.

Eva Hoffman (1998) described the feeling of loss and being lost during her childhood emigration from Poland to Canada as being like a plant with its roots exposed. She struggled to make meaning of her new experiences and found that she initially lacked the language to even explain the meaning of her new life to herself. Her internal logic was gone at first, but then returned stronger in a way she described as retaining "the capacity for attachment" (Hoffman, 1998, p. 75) with her past while striking out to form new ways of bringing logical pattern to abstract, and at times overwhelming, information.

Mary Catherine Bateson, a writer and cultural anthropologist, advised that, like Quixote, the knight errant is a good model to follow in times of heavy information processing and often overwhelming discontinuity (Bateson, 1990). The ability to improvise and compose one's way through the challenges of life can bring a powerful fluidity and sense of achievement, even if things happen that are sometimes considered failures (Bateson, 1990). Bateson's writing focused on the value of improvisational ability in the face of mental hardship. Those of us who work in the field can see that improvisational ability in many study abroad students' attempts to make meaning out of what they must face overseas. The temptation to protect oneself from this shock, as Hoffman had been advised by her piano instructor, and as Wexler described as a common reaction for new arrivals in foreign lands, is strong and unavoidable for some.

But for those who, like Sancho Panza, proceed and struggle when things no longer make sense, and who, like Hoffman, recognize initial cognitive inabilities as launching pads to higher levels of reasoning, the journey can be as progressive as it is uncomfortable, especially to the first timer who is not yet so worldly. For the person who, like Bateson, is willing and able to reconsider the role of authorities in determining right and wrong, the international experience could provide the setting for her or him to begin making her or his own meaning out of confrontation with diversity, because it is unavoidable.

This research study found evidence for a phenomenon I call "the first time effect," that college students who lacked meaningful international exposure before studying abroad began at a lower level of intellectual development than their peers, but that this gap disappeared after a semester abroad. If that first international experience is so searing and impactful that it leads to such a gain, then it deserves greater attention for what it can reveal about the nature of international experiences and intellectual development.

"Take heed, brother Sancho, that this adventure and others of this kind are not adventures of islands but crossroads" (Cervantes, 1957).

APPENDIX A.1

Schools Involved in the Study

For all of the schools mentioned, students from both their own college and from other colleges enroll in that school's study abroad programs. I chose these schools for several reasons. First, they were institutions where I had personal or professional affiliations that allowed me to seriously approach my contact for the purpose of enlisting his or her help. Second, they are study abroad departments that I knew typically enrolled cumulatively over 1,000 students in a given semester, which was a large enough number that I could reasonably hope to be successful attracting many students to my study. Third, they are departments that manage study abroad programs in all parts of the English-speaking and non-English-speaking world, and with both study center and direct placement programs, two of my research variables.

Schools participating in the research study included:

- SUNY Albany
- SUNY Binghamton
- SUNY Brockport
- SUNY Cortland
- SUNY New Paltz
- SUNY Oswego
- SUNY Plattsburgh
- Syracuse University

APPENDIX A.2

Institutional Review Board Results

Where necessary, a separate Institutional Review Board (IRB) application was submitted to participating campus human subjects committees. In the remaining cases, approval at my institution was accepted as sufficient. The chart below indicates where a separate IRB application was required, and the results of that process:

School	IRB Application Date	Result
SUNY Oswego	7/23/03	Approval, 9/8/03
Syracuse University	8/12/03	Approval, 10/16/03
SUNY Plattsburgh	8/26/03	Approval, 10/15/03
SUNY New Paltz	9/22/03	Approval, 11/3/03
SUNY Albany	11/15/03	Approval, 12/10/03

Of special note is that these approvals were granted with the understanding that students would be participating in an online research project and could not sign a standard informed consent statement. In each case, I supplied the IRB with copies of my research Web site pages, with the explanation that the "Submit" button would be the equivalent of the student's signature granting informed consent. No IRB had an objection to this survey format or online proof of informed consent.

Script for Participating Schools

I sent the following sample recruiting script to my contacts at the other schools for the purpose of inviting their students to participate prior to studying abroad. The same script (modified) and method were used to invite students to participate at the end of their study abroad semester:

> You are being asked to take part in a brief online research study of spring 2004 semester study abroad students. Your participation is completely voluntary, but we encourage you to participate as it will help us learn more about study abroad as a vehicle for student learning. As an incentive, students who take part in the study are eligible to win a gift certificate from Amazon.com.
>
> Please visit the following site
>
> http://www.studyabroad.homestead.com
>
> to participate. The survey and essay are in the "Take Survey Here" section. Please complete your participation before you leave for your study abroad semester. Thank you!

APPENDIX B

Pilot Test and Follow-up Testing

I conducted a pilot test to determine whether a Web site would be suitable for conducting this research. Starting in the summer of 2003, I sent a brief e-mail request and the Web site link to a pilot group of 20 students who were leaving for study abroad programs in the fall of 2003. The students were representative of my study variables of gender and program structure. Of those 20, 4 replied with feedback. During that fall, before going live with the research Web site, I also sent the site to the faculty members and study abroad administrators who agreed to assist me, and to the coordinator of the Center for the Study of Intellectual Development (CSID) for feedback.

Feedback from the pilot was generally positive. Students liked the layout and did not report any difficulty in taking the survey itself, or in understanding how to use the Web site. One student reported a problem using a Web browser (a Linux-based browser) other than Internet Explorer (IE) or Netscape Navigator. Also, the CSID coordinator indicated that the Web site did not work as well on his Mac computer. For these reasons, and since I had noticed that the layout and speed of the site were better on IE, I added the following statement to the main page and to the survey page: "For best results, please use Internet Explorer (IE) on a PC, not a Mac."

One student commented that after he submitted his survey he would prefer to see some automatic communication from the Web site indicating that his survey had been received. He said that he did not feel confident that it had gone through without this. I researched the site service provider's Web site and found a way to add this feature. Another student suggested that I use the term "Home College" in addition to asking where students are enrolled. He thought "Home College" was clearer. I added this additional wording to the online form. Another student said that when she tried to e-mail me using one of the e-mail links that I had inserted,

131

it did not work. I fixed that problem. Other suggestions were to allow participants to tab through the questions in order and to indicate very clearly where on the site the survey section is. I made those changes.

On the subject of the MID essay prompt, two pilot respondents said that they felt that being asked to write for "about 20 minutes" was too long and might discourage students from participating. One student said she was finished in 10 minutes. I communicated directly with the coordinator of the CSID, asking him whether students needed to write for a definite length of time, or if it would be better to ask students to submit an essay with a certain word count. His reply was that the quality, thoughtfulness, and seriousness of the writing were more important than any word count or length of time (personal communication, October 19, 2003). Since one student had suggested 10 minutes, I decided to change the Web site, asking students to write for "about 10–15 minutes." The CSID coordinator also required that I add his contact information to my site, with the statement that the MID essay prompt should not be copied or distributed without the written consent of the CSID.

APPENDIX C

Questionnaire

1. Name: _____ (first, middle, last)

2. E-mail address: _____

3. Gender: [check one]   ☐ Female   ☐ Male

4. What year were you born?: _____

5. I am a: [check one]   ☐ senior
                          ☐ junior
                          ☐ sophomore
                          ☐ freshman

6. What is your major? (Write "undeclared" if you have not declared a major.) _____

7. What is your grade point average (GPA)? _____

8. In which country will you (did you) study abroad?

   _____

9. At what college or university are you enrolled (your home college)? _____

10. What college or university administered your study abroad program? [check one]

    ☐ SUNY Albany   ☐ SUNY Binghamton
    ☐ SUNY New Paltz   ☐ SUNY Oswego
    ☐ SUNY Plattsburgh   ☐ SUNY Cortland
    ☐ Syracuse University ☐ SUNY Brockport   ☐ other

11. Have you traveled abroad before?: ☐ Yes ☐ No

    (For post-students: *Before study abroad*, had you traveled abroad before?)

If yes, how long was your longest trip abroad?

_____

(12–13 below for pre-students only)

*12. What got you interested in study abroad? [check all that apply]

- ☐ I wanted to learn another language.
- ☐ I thought it would be fun.
- ☐ I thought it would be good for my career.
- ☐ I wanted to travel.
- ☐ My parents encouraged it.
- ☐ Professors encouraged it.
- ☐ My friends were doing it.
- ☐ I wanted an adventure.
- ☐ I wanted to learn about other cultures.
- ☐ It was good for my major.
- ☐ I thought it would make me a better person.
- ☐ Other _____

*13. A lot of students don't study abroad because of certain concerns they have about it. What were some of your concerns about study abroad? [check all that apply]

- ☐ Financial concerns
- ☐ Parents' concerns
- ☐ Didn't want to travel
- ☐ Credit transfer problems
- ☐ Didn't want to be away from home campus
- ☐ Didn't feel comfortable
- ☐ Didn't want to fall behind in my major
- ☐ Other _____
- ☐ I had no concerns.

(12–14 below for post-students only)

12. When you studied abroad, which of the following best describes the other students in your classes?: [*choose one*]

- ☐ Most of the other students in my classes were NOT from the United States.

☐ Most of the other students in my classes were from the United States.

13. Which of the following best describes where you lived while abroad?: [*choose one*]

☐ With a host family
☐ In a residence hall or apartment with people NOT from the United States
☐ In a residence hall or apartment with other American students

14. Did you participate in any of the activities below while abroad?: [*check all that apply to you*]

☐ Looked for and found my own housing
☐ A practicum, internship, field experience, co-op, student teaching, etc.
☐ Community service or volunteer work
☐ Worked on a project that had regular interaction with host country people or organizations
☐ Joined a club, group, or activity with mostly host country students
☐ A language practice group or other academic activity with host country students
☐ Had serious conversations with students or others from the host country

(List any other activities in which you participated with PEOPLE FROM THE HOST COUNTRY.)

*Results from these questions were not researched for this study but rather were of general interest to me as a study abroad professional.

APPENDIX D

Pilot Research Project Results

In the summer of 2001 I conducted a small study (n = 26) to pilot what would become this larger study. That initial study yielded some evidence that suggested that study abroad can be one of the challenging and "disequilibriating" experiences in which a college student can participate that fosters intellectual development. Gains in intellectual development scores for students taking part in study abroad programs, as scored on the Measure of Intellectual Development (MID), were observed. These significant differences existed for both male and female students, and for students participating in study abroad programs in both of the countries studied (Spain and China) at the .05 level (McKeown, 2005).

APPENDIX E

Study Limitations

This research study was an exploratory study of the impact of studying abroad on college student intellectual development. The students participating in the study were not necessarily representative of all students who study abroad, or of all students who attend college at the universities involved in the study. This research examined students who self-selected to study abroad for one semester and who self-selected participating in the study. Therefore, conclusions should be made with caution when comparing students in this study with those studying abroad at other schools, or with college students generally.

This was an exploratory study of one semester's study abroad participants studying through several university-based study abroad programs. These programs were administered by public and private universities at small and large campuses and enrolled students from outside of the universities performing the administration. The findings of this study reflect the voluntary responses of those students participating in the study.

In this research study all students studying abroad through the participating universities were invited to participate, but it must be remembered that these students all self-selected studying abroad. Those students who participated in this study did so voluntarily, while some others did not agree to participate, and still others participated only in either the pre- or post-portions of the study.

This study made no attempt to rate the quality of program delivery for the many different study abroad programs whose students became part of the study. Broad differences in the program structure and broad categories of the program offerings (such as the language of the host country) were identified, but the success with which the programs were delivered and the quality of the program components were not studied. Therefore, it was possible to categorize student participation into defined program types, but it was not possible to understand how well those programs were designed and delivered.

Limitations of the Sample

The composition and size of the sample were limitations of this study. Including my own SUNY Oswego students, the schools that agreed to participate in this study sent abroad over 1,800 students during the spring 2004 semester. However, because participation in the study was voluntary, not every student participated. An effort was made to obtain a large sample of data representative of the study abroad population. However, I relied on very busy colleagues in study abroad offices, and possibly inaccurate student records, as the source of access to most of my proposed student subjects. This, most likely, affected my response rate. It also should be noted that even though I provided my study abroad colleagues at the other schools with a script to follow, inconsistent methods were likely used to recruit students.

It also is possible that my response rate was affected by my choice to survey students from a distance. I attempted to reach a large number of students through multiple schools, but I did so through distant, perhaps even detached, methods such as mailings, e-mails, and a Web site. It was not the use of a Web-based survey per se that caused less than full participation, I believe, but rather that I was unable to control tightly the administration conditions at the various study abroad sites. It is possible, of course, that some students were simply not interested in participating.

In addition, the sample itself was not random. Self-selection was made by the participants at every stage of the study. I presented in chapter 3 the results of a proxy analysis of the students in this study and compared them to certain characteristics of the study abroad population from these schools and nationwide, as gathered by the Institute of International Education (2003) in its annual Open Doors survey, and other research studies (Martin, 1987; Martin & Rohrlich, 1991) and sources (Monalco, 2002). In this way I was able to examine whether the students in this study sample were representative of study abroad students more broadly on characteristics such as gender, previous international travel, program structure, and the language of the study abroad country. While there is no way to prevent completely self-selection artifacts from biasing the study, I made an effort to compare these students to other study abroad students in these programs and nationally. This study's conclusions should be viewed as having been presented in as generalizable a manner as possible, given the constraints of time, financial resources, and access to students.

Attributes of Study Abroad Students

It should be noted that the focus of this research study was not to compare study abroad students with those not participating. However, to explore further the question of the generalizability of the results, it is important to note that any gains seen in intellectual development when studying abroad may or may not be caused by the study abroad experience itself. Since study abroad students are self-selected, it is possible that the attributes of those students who self-select to study abroad also could explain the outcomes. This problem of self-selection could affect the generalizability of the research as applied to college students overall if those students not studying abroad do not possess those same attributes.

Whitt, Edison, Pascarella, Terenzini, and Nora (2001) argued that certain student characteristics can influence the outcome being studied. This problem could have affected the results of this study, because any gains in intellectual development while studying abroad may reflect the characteristics of the students themselves, whether or not they went on a study abroad program. This may happen because researchers (Fischer & Silvern, 1985) believe that individual differences in intellectual reasoning come about by an individual interacting with a particular context and exhibiting competent cognitive abilities in that context. Without the same context and the same individual, the outcome might be different, because that same person in a different context might not be ready or "primed" (Fischer & Silvern, 1985, p. 621).

Research comparing study abroad students with those not going abroad is limited. One research study examining personality differences between study abroad students and those not going abroad found that students who study abroad tend to seek out different and more nonconformist experiences while in college, and that they also tend to show a greater willingness to work hard, to choose difficult tasks, and to compete against others (Schroth & McCormack, 2000). These results were true for both female and male study abroad students and suggest that study abroad students may seek challenging experiences, and work hard at them, more so than their peers who do not study abroad (Schroth & McCormack, 2000). Since no attempt was made in this research study to compare participating students with nonstudy abroad participants, the results of this study should be viewed as pertaining to study abroad students with some support and encouragement for nonstudy abroad participants.

Duration of Study

The time period chosen for study, one semester of study abroad, was considered relevant by the researcher, since it is the most popular duration for study abroad (IIE, 2004) and because researchers in intellectual development (Moore, 1990) have observed gains over that length of time. Some researchers in higher education (Baxter Magolda, 1992) have used longitudinal studies that include post-graduation analyses when studying intellectual development. Similarly, the delayed impact of study abroad has been suggested by international education researchers (Vande Berg et al., 2004). It is possible that for some students one semester of study abroad was not of sufficient length to observe any gains in intellectual development.

Study Abroad as Treatment

This study was a preliminary investigation into the impact of studying abroad on student intellectual development. While I attempted to include as many variables as feasible in order to gain a fuller understanding of intellectual development on studying abroad, there are several areas in which further research is necessary to support any conclusions. Particularly, this research was an attempt to study students taking part in one-semester study abroad programs, not full-year programs or short-term or summer programs.

Studying abroad as a treatment suitable to be associated with gains in intellectual development for all participating students was unproven. This research sought to know more about this possibility. Research in intellectual development (King, 1990; Perry, 1968) has shown that it occurs in interaction with the environment, and that failure to develop could result from the lack of environmental opportunities (Mines, et al., 1990). Further, research using the MID instrument has shown that the biggest gains typically come in a student's first year and just before graduation (W. S. Moore, personal communication, April 27, 2005). Study abroad participation rates nationally, and participants' characteristics for this study, indicate still that mostly juniors study abroad. While the variables chosen for research, particularly regarding the program structure and the language of the country, were done so with the hope of identifying environmental factors when studying abroad, it is not evident that these variables in program structure are conducive toward fostering intellectual development. Only one variable, previous international travel experience, was associated with intellectual developmental differences in participating students.

References

Aczel, A. D. (1993). *Complete business statistics.* Homewood, IL: Irwin.

Adler, P. S. (1975, Fall). The transitional experience: An alternative view of culture shock. *Journal of Humanistic Psychology, 15 (4)*, 13–23.

Anderson, A. (2003, Fall). Women and cultural learning in Costa Rica: Reading the contexts. *Frontiers: The Interdisciplinary Journal of Study Abroad, 21–52.*

Anderson, L. (1995). A new look at an old construct: Cross-cultural adaptation. *International Journal of Intercultural Relations, 18*, 293–328.

Astin, A. W. (1984, July). Student involvement: A developmental theory for higher education. *Journal of College Student Personnel*, 297–308.

Babbie, E. (1990). *Survey research methods*, 2d ed. Belmont, CA: Wadsworth.

Bateson, M. C. (1990). *Composing a life.* New York: Plume/Penguin.

Baxter Magolda, M. (1992). *Knowing and reasoning in college: Gender related patterns in students' intellectual development.* San Francisco: Jossey-Bass.

Beach, R. (1995). *Multicultural learning at home and abroad.* Grant No. P116B20204–94. Washington, DC: Fund for the Improvement of Postsecondary Education. ERIC Document Reproduction Service No. ED 415 791.

Belenky, M. F., Clinchy, B. M., Goldberger, N. R., & Tarule, J. M. (1986). *Women's ways of knowing: The development of self, voice, and mind.* New York: BasicBooks.

Birnbaum, R. (1988). *How colleges work: The cybernetics of academic organization and leadership.* San Francisco: Jossey-Bass.

Bochner, S. (1982). The social psychology of cross-cultural relations. In S. Bochner (Ed.), *Cultures in contact: Studies in cross-cultural interaction* (pp. 5–44). Oxford: Pergamon Press.

145

Card, K. A., & Horton, L. (2000). Providing access to graduate education using computer-mediated communication. *International Journal of Instructional Media, 27 (3)*, 235–245.

Carlson, J. S., Burn, B. B., Useem, J., & Yachimowicz, D. (1990). *Study abroad: The experience of American undergraduates*. New York: Greenwood Press.

Cervantes, M. (1957). *Don Quixote of La Mancha*, translated by Walter Starkie. London: Macmillan.

Chickering, A. (1969). *Education and identity*. San Francisco: Jossey-Bass.

Christie, R. A.. & Ragans, S. W. (1999, Summer). Beyond borders: A model for student and staff development. In J. C. Dalton (Ed.), *New directions for student services, 86. Beyond borders: How international developments are changing student affairs practice* (pp. 79–87). San Francisco: Jossey-Bass.

Citron, J. (1995, March). Can cross-cultural understanding aid second language acquisition? Toward a theory of ethno-lingual relativity. *Hispania, 78*, 105–113.

Citron, J. (1996, June). *Short-term study abroad: Integration, third culture formation, and re-entry*. Paper presented at the NAFSA Annual Conference, Phoenix, Arizona.

Couper, M. P. (2000). Web surveys: A review of issues and approaches. *Public Opinion Quarterly, 64 (4)*, 464–494.

Cress, C. M., Astin, H. S., Zimmerman-Oster, K., & Burkhardt, J. C. (2001). Developmental outcomes of college students' involvement in leadership activities. *Journal of College Student Development, 42 (1)*, 15–27.

Dewey, J. (1916). *Democracy and education: An introduction to the philosophy of education*. New York: Macmillan.

De Wit, H. (1997). Studies in international education: A research perspective. *Journal of Studies in International Education, 1 (1)*, 1–8.

Dey, E. L. (1997). Undergraduate political attitudes: Peer influence in changing social contexts. *Journal of Higher Education, 68 (4)*, 398–413.

Doughty, C. (1987). Relating second-language acquisition theory to CALL research and application. In W. F. Smith (Ed.), *Modern media in foreign language education: Theory and implementation* (pp. 133–167). Lincolnwood, IL: National Textbook Company.

Douglas, C., & Jones-Rikkers, C. G. (2001). Study abroad programs and American student worldmindedness: An empirical analysis. *Journal of Teaching in International Business, 13 (1)*, 55–66.

Douglas, N. L. (2000). Enemies of critical thinking: Lessons from social psychology research. *Reading Psychology, 21*, 129–144.

Drews, D. ., Meyer, L. L., & Peregrine, P. N. (1996, December). Effects of study abroad on conceptualizations of national groups. *College Student Journal, 30 (4)*, 452–461.

Engle, L., & Engle, J. (2003, Fall). Study abroad levels: Toward a classification of program types. *Frontiers: The Interdisciplinary Journal of Study Abroad*, 1–20.

Ennis, R. H. (1993, Summer). Critical thinking assessment. *Theory into Practice, 32 (3)*, 179–186.

Farrell, P., & Suvedi, M. (2003, Fall). Studying abroad in Nepal: Assessing impact. *Frontiers: The Interdisciplinary Journal of Study Abroad*, 175–188.

Feinberg, B. (2002, May 3). What students don't learn abroad. *The Chronicle of Higher Education, 48*, B20.

Ferguson, N. (2001). Clashing civilizations or mad mullahs: The United States between informal and formal empire. In S. Talbott & N. Chanda (Eds.), *The age of terror: America and the world after September 11* (pp. 113–141). New York: Basic Books.

Fischer, K. W., & Silvern, L. (1985). Stages and individual differences in cognitive development. *Annual Review of Psychology, 36*, 613–648.

Flowers, L., & Pascarella, E. T. (1999). Cognitive effects of college racial composition on African American students after 3 years of college. *Journal of College Student Development, 40 (6)*, 669–677.

Furnham, A., & Bochner, S. (1986). *Culture shock: Psychological reactions to unfamiliar environments*. London: Routledge.

Gerner, M., Perry, F., Moselle, M. A., & Archbold, M. (1992). Characteristics of internationally mobile adolescents. *Journal of School Psychology, 30 (2)*, 197–214.

Hancock, D. R., & Flowers, C. P. (2001). Comparing social desirability responding on world wide web and paper-administered surveys. *Educational Technology Research and Development, 49 (1)*, 5–13.

Hansel, B., & Grove, N. (1986). International student exchange programs—Are the educational benefits real? *NASSP Bulletin, 70 (487)*, 84–90.

Herman, S. (1970). *American students in Israel*. Ithaca, NY: Cornell University Press.

Hoffa, W.W. (2007). *A history of US study abroad: Beginnings to 1965*. Carlisle, PA: The Forum on Education Abroad.

Hoffman, E. (1998). *Lost in translation*. London: Vintage UK Random House.

Horn, L., Peter, K, & Rooney, K. (2002, Fall). Profile of undergraduates in U.S. postsecondary education institutions: 1999–2000. *Education Statistics Quarterly, 4 (3)*, 79–86.

Huebner, L. A., & Lawson, J. M. (1990). Understanding and assessing college environments. In D.G. Creamer & Associates (Eds.), *College student development: Theory and practice for the 1990's* (pp. 127–151). Lanham, MD: American College Personnel Association.

Hull, W. F., IV. (1978). *Foreign students in the United States of America: Coping behavior within the educational environment*. New York: Praeger.

Institute of International Education. (2003). *Open doors: Report on international educational exchange 2003*. New York: Institute of International Education.

Institute of International Education. (2004). *Open doors: Report on international educational exchange 2004*. New York: Institute of International Education.

Institute of International Education. (2005). *Open doors: Report on international educational exchange 2005*. New York: Institute of International Education.

Institute of International Education. (2006). *Open doors: Report on international educational exchange 2006*. New York: Institute of International Education.

Jacoby, B., & Associates (1996). *Service-learning in higher education: Concepts and practices*. San Francisco: Jossey-Bass.

Kauffmann, N. L., & Kuh, G. D. (1984, April). *The impact of study abroad on personal development of college students.* Paper presented at the meeting of the American Educational Research Association, New Orleans, Louisiana.

Kauffmann, N. L., Martin, J. N., Weaver, H. D., & Weaver, J. (1992). *Students abroad: Strangers at home.* Yarmouth, ME: Intercultural Press.

Kerr, C. W. (1985). Foreword. In W. Allaway & H. Shorrock (Eds.), *Dimensions of international higher education: The University of California symposium on education abroad* (pp. xiii–xvi). Boulder, CO: Westview Press.

Kim, Y. Y. (1988). *Communication and cross-cultural adaptation.* Philadelphia: Multilingual Matters.

King, P. M. (1978). William Perry's theory of intellectual and ethical development. In L. Knefelkamp, C. Widick, & C. Parker (Eds.), *Applying new developmental findings* (pp. 35–51). San Francisco: Jossey-Bass.

King, P. M. (1990). Assessing development from a cognitive-developmental perspective. In D. G. Creamer & Associates (Eds.), *College student development: Theory and practice for the 1990's* (pp. 81–96). Lanham, MD: American College Personnel Association.

Knefelkamp, L., Widick, C., & Parker, C. A. (1978). Editor's notes: Why bother with theory? In L. Knefelkamp, C. Widick, & C. Parker (Eds.), *Applying new developmental findings* (pp. 79–91). San Francisco: Jossey-Bass.

Knefelkamp, L. (2003). The influence of a classic. *Liberal Education, 89 (3),* 10–15.

Kohlberg, L. (1971). Stages of moral development. In C. M. Beck, B. S. Crittenden, & E. V. Sullivan (Eds.), *Moral education* (pp. 30–41). Toronto: University of Toronto Press.

Kohlberg, L. (1980). Stages of moral development as a basis for moral education. In B. Munsey (Ed.), *Moral development, moral education, and Kohlberg: Basic issues in philosophy, psychology, religion, and education* (pp. 15–98). Birmingham, AL: Religious Education Press.

Kolb, D. A. (1984). *Experiential learning.* Englewood Cliffs, NJ: Prentice Hall.

Koveos, P., & Tang, L. (2004, Special Issue). Offshore outsourcing: Japan, Europe and the rest of the world. *Indian Journal of Economics & Business,* 43–62.

Kuh, G. D. (1995). The other curriculum: Out-of-class experiences associated with student learning and personal development. *Journal of Higher Education, 66 (2)*, 123–155.

Marcum, J. A. (2001, May 18). Eliminate the roadblocks. *The Chronicle of Higher Education*, B7–8.

Marion, P. B. (1980, January). Relationships of student characteristics and experiences with attitude changes in a program of study abroad. *Journal of College Student Personnel*, 58–64.

Martin, J. N. (1987). The relationship between student sojourner perceptions of intercultural competencies and previous sojourn experience. *International Journal of Intercultural Relations, 11*, 337–355.

Martin, J. N., & Rohrlich, B. (1991). The relationship between study-abroad student expectations and selected student characteristics. *Journal of College Student Development, 32*, 39–46.

Martin, L. M. (2000). The relationship of college experiences to psychosocial outcomes in students. *Journal of College Student Development, 41 (3)*, 292–301.

McKeown, J. S. (2003). The impact of September 11 on study abroad student interest and concern: An exploratory study. *International Education, 32 (2)*, 85–95.

McKeown, J. S. (2005). Measuring intellectual development of U.S. study abroad students. *Educacion Global: Asociacion Mexicana para la Educacion Internacional, 9*, 33–39.

McKeown, J. S., & Nekritz, T. (2006, Fall). Harnessing the ambient currents: The opportunities, challenges, and progression of initiating a short-term program. *IIE Networker: The International Education Magazine*, 35–37.

McNamee, S. J., & Faulkner, G. L. (2001, Spring). The international exchange experience and the social construction of meaning. *Journal of Studies in International Education, 5 (1)*, 64–78.

Medina-Lopez-Portillo, A. (2004, Fall). Intercultural learning assessment: The link between program duration and the development of intercultural sensitivity. *Frontiers: The Interdisciplinary Journal of Study Abroad*, 179–199.

Miller, E. J. (1993, February). *Culture shock: A student's perspective of study abroad and the importance of promoting study abroad programs.* Paper presented at the Tenth Annual Intercultural and International Communication Conference, Miami, Florida.

Mines, R. A., King, P. M., Hood, A. B., & Wood, P. K. (1990). Stages of intellectual development and associated critical thinking skills in college students. *Journal of College Student Development, 31*, 538–547.

Monalco. (2002). *Survey of third party study abroad providers: Final report.* Milwaukee, WI: Monalco.

Moore, W. S. (1989). The Learning Environment Preferences: Exploring the construct validity of an objective measure of the Perry scheme of intellectual development. *Journal of College Student Development, 30*, 504–514.

Moore, W. S. (1990). *The measure of intellectual development (MID): An instrument manual.* Olympia, WA: Center for the Study of Intellectual Development.

Moore, W. S. (1999). *Interpreting MID ratings.* Olympia, WA: Center for the Study of Intellectual Development.

NAFSA: Association of International Educators. (2003). Strategic plan. Washington, DC: NAFSA.

National Survey of Student Engagement. (2000). The college student report. Bloomington, IN: Indiana University Center for Postsecondary Research and Planning.

NSSE: National Survey of Student Engagement. (2007). Experiences that matter: Enhancing student learning and success. Bloomington, IN: Center for Postsecondary Research, School of Education, Indiana University, Bloomington.

Oberg, K. (1960). Culture shock: Adjustment to new cultural environments. *Practical Anthropology, 7*, 177–182.

Opello, W. C., & Rosow, S. J. (2004). *The nation-state and global order: A historical introduction to contemporary politics.* Boulder, CO: Lynne Rienner.

Pascarella, E. T. (2001). Using student self-reported gains to estimate college impact: A cautionary tale. *Journal of College Student Development, 42 (5)*, 488–492.

Pascarella, E. T., Palmer, B., Moye, M., & Pierson, C. T. (2001). Do diversity experiences influence the development of critical thinking? *Journal of College Student Development, 42 (3)*, 257–271.

Pedersen, P. (1995). *The five stages of culture shock: Critical incidents around the world.* Westport, CT: Greenwood Press.

Perry, W. G., Jr. (1968). *Forms of intellectual and ethical development in the college years: A scheme.* Cambridge, MA: President and Fellows of Harvard College.

Petress, K. (2004, Spring). Critical thinking: An extended definition. *Education, 124 (3),* 461–466.

Piaget, J. (1965). *The moral judgment of the child.* New York: Free Press.

Poggi, G. (1990). *The state: Its nature, development, and prospects.* Stanford, CA: Stanford University Press.

Rest, J. (1980). Developmental psychology and value education. In B. Munsey (Ed.), *Moral development, moral education, and Kohlberg: Basic issues in philosophy, psychology, religion, and education* (pp. 101–129). Birmingham, AL: Religious Education Press.

Rivers, W. P. (1998). Is being there enough? The effects of homestay placements on language gain during study abroad. *Foreign Language Annals, 31 (4),* 492–500.

Roochnik, D. (2001, May 18). First, look homeward. *The Chronicle of Higher Education,* B9–10.

Sanford, N. (1962). *The American college: A psychological and social interpretation of the higher learning.* New York: John Wiley & Sons.

Sanford, N. (1966). *Self and society: Social change and individual development.* New York: Atherton.

Sanford, N. (1967). *Where colleges fail: A study of the student as a person.* San Francisco: Jossey-Bass.

Schaefer, D. R., & Dillman, D. A. (1998). Development of standards e-mail methodology: Results of an experiment. *Public Opinion Quarterly, 62 (3),* 378–397.

Schonland, A. M., & Williams, P. W. (1996). Using the Internet for travel and tourism survey research: Experiences from the Net traveler survey. *Journal of Travel Research, 35 (2),* 81–87.

Schroth, M. L., & McCormack, W. A. (2000). Sensation seeking and need for achievement among study-abroad students. *The Journal of Social Psychology, 140 (4),* 533–535.

Sharma, M. P., & Mulka, J. S. (1993, March). *The impact of international education upon United States students in comparative perspective.* Paper presented at Comparative and International Education Society 1993 Annual Conference, Kingston, Jamaica.

Shaw, K. A. (1999). *The successful president: "BuzzWords" on leadership.* Phoenix, AZ: American Council on Education/Oryx Press.

Smith, W. F. (1987). Modern media in foreign language education: A synopsis. In W. F. Smith (Ed.), *Modern media in foreign language education: Theory and implementation* (pp. 1–12). Lincolnwood, IL: National Textbook Company.

State University of New York. (2004). SUNY study abroad program internal materials: Overseas program enrollments.

Storti, C. (1990). *The art of crossing cultures.* Yarmouth, ME: Intercultural Press.

Sutton, R. C., & Rubin, D. L. (2004, Fall). The GLOSSARI project: Initial findings from a system-wide research initiative on study abroad learning outcomes. *Frontiers: The Interdisciplinary Journal of Study Abroad*, 65–82.

Syracuse University. (2001). A strategic partnership for innovative research and education (A-SPIRE): An Academic Plan for Syracuse University.

The Forum on Education Abroad. (2003). 2002–03 Annual Report. The Forum on Education Abroad: http://www.forumea.org.

Thot, I. D. (1998). *The Congress-Bundestag youth exchange for young professionals: What are the effects on U.S. students? An executive summary.* Claremont, CA: Claremont Graduate University Center for International Studies.

Tinto, V. (1987). *Leaving college: Rethinking the causes and cures of student attrition.* Chicago: University of Chicago Press.

Tinto, V. (1993). *Leaving college: Rethinking the causes and cures of student attrition.* Chicago: University of Chicago Press.

Tse, A. C. (1998). Comparing the response rate, speed, and response quality of two methods of sending questionnaires: E-mail vs. mail. *Journal of the Market Research Society, 40 (4)*, 353–361.

U.S. Department of Education. (2000). Strengthening the U.S. government's leadership in promoting international education: A Discussion Paper. Washington, DC: U.S. Department of Education.

154 *References*

Vande Berg, M. J., Balkcum, A., Scheid, M., & Whalen, B. J. (2004, Fall). The Georgetown University Consortium Project: A report at the halfway mark. *Frontiers: The Interdisciplinary Journal of Study Abroad*, 101–116.

Van Hoof, H. B., & Verbeeten, M. J. (2005). Wine is for drinking, water is for washing: Student opinions about international exchange programs. *Journal of Studies in International Education, 9 (1)*, 42–61.

Vygotsky, L. S. (1978). *Mind in society: The development of higher psychological processes.* Cambridge, MA: Harvard University Press.

Walker, D. A. (1999). The organization and administration of study abroad centers in two institutions. *International Education, 29 (1)*, 5–15.

Wexler, B. E. (2006). *Brain and culture: Neurobiology, ideology, and social change.* Cambridge, MA: MIT Press.

Whitt, E. J., Edison, M. I., Pascarella, E. T., Terenzini, P. T., & Nora, A. (2001). Influences on students' openness to diversity and challenge in the second and third years of college. *The Journal of Higher Education, 72 (2)*, 172–204.

Widick, C., Parker, C. A., & Knefelkamp, L. (1978). Douglas Heath's model of maturing. In L. Knefelkamp, C. Widick, & C. Parker (Eds.), *Applying new developmental findings* (pp. 79–91). San Francisco: Jossey-Bass.

Index